How this book will help you
by David Walton and Trevor Green

KV-011-111

Key focus – Exam skills and technique

This book will help you to improve your performance in AS General Studies, whichever board's exam you are sitting. It is not so much concerned with the knowledge you require – this should be covered in your course – it is about the **skills** you will be called upon to demonstrate in the exam.

There are **four different specifications** set by the three main boards: **AQA A, AQA B, Edexcel** and **OCR**. The exams are different in a number of ways, but the content and question styles overlap. **General Studies exams are mainly about skills** and, as the Assessment Objectives are common for all specifications (see page 7), it is the same sets of skills which are being assessed, even though some of the question types or styles may differ (see pages 4–5). Practising these key exam skills is what the book is all about.

Three main sections to this book

There are three main sections to this book, which relate to the **three main topic areas** of AS General Studies. These are:

Unit 1:	Culture, Morality, Arts and Humanities
Unit 2:	Science, Mathematics and Technology
Unit 3:	Society, Politics and the Economy.

(In **AQA B** the titles of the units are different (e.g. *Conflict*, *Power* and *Space*), but you will find AQA B style questions in each section of the book.)

Questions for all specifications

We have categorised the exam questions set for all four specifications into a number of different types (see grid on pages 4–5) Each of the three sections in this book includes examples of these different types of questions. Some of the questions test more than one aspect or skill. **Using the grid, you can easily find and use the questions relevant to your particular specification.** However, even though some of the question styles may be different from the ones you have to answer (e.g. not every board has multiple-choice questions), it may still be worth working through these, as they are broadly testing the same understanding and skills and this will give you extra practice.

Examination questions, Students' answers and 'How to score full marks'

The first part of each section in this book consists of **typical questions followed by students' answers.** We have then written a detailed commentary, **'How to score full marks'** which highlights where marks are gained and lost. There are also **'Don't forget …'** boxes that summarise essential aspects of exam technique.

Questions to try, Model answers and Examiner's comments

The second part of each section contains questions of different types for you to try. At the end of the book you will find model answers to each of the questions. These are answers that would score full marks, which you can compare against your own answers. We have provided comments on why these are particularly good answers.

Question types and exam skills

Question type number in this book	Description of question type/exam skill	AQA A units	AQA B units	Edexcel units	OCR units	Page numbers in this book
1	Knowledge and understanding of topics – multiple choice (MC)	1,2		2		11–13, 27–28, 33–36, 37, 45–52, 55–56, 79
2	Knowledge and understanding of topics – short answer (SA)		1	1,2,3	2,3	19, 29, 37, 38, 40–42, 57
3	Knowledge and understanding of topics – essay		2	1,2,3	1,2,3	20–21, 22–23, 29, 40–42, 43–44, 57, 73–74, 75–77, 81
4	Comprehension of sources – multiple choice	1,2		3		11–13, 27–28, 33–36, 55–56
Comprehension of sources – short answer/extended writing:						
5	Summarise/outline contents	1,3			1,3	15–16, 29, 63–64
6	Analyse/interpret information	1,3			1,3	17, 29, 57, 62, 63–64, 65–66, 71–72, 78, 80
7	Explain/discuss/develop ideas	1,3	2		1,3	17, 19, 22–23, 29, 57, 71–72, 73–74, 75–77, 81
8	Comment on/construct arguments	1,3	2,3	1,2,3	1,3	20–21, 22–23, 29, 57, 65–66, 69–70, 71–72, 73–74, 75–77, 80–81
9	Assess knowledge/purpose/value	1,3	2,3	1,2,3	1,3	18, 22–23. 29, 38, 41–42, 43–44, 57, 69–70, 71–72, 80
10	Recognise differences/limitations/bias	1,3	2,3	1,2,3	1,3	18, 20–21, 22–23, 29, 38, 41–42, 43–44, 57, 65–66, 71–71, 80
11	Draw conclusions	1,3	2,3	1,2,3	1,3	20–21, 22–23, 29, 41–42, 43–44, 57, 69–70, 71–72, 73–74, 75–77, 80–81
	Respond to data:	(MC)	(SA)	(SA)	(SA)	
12	Perform calculations	2	3	3	2,3	37, 39, 45–52, 57, 59, 61–79
13	Construct/analyse graphs and diagrams	2	3	3	2,3	33–36, 45–52
14	Identify/comment on trends	2	3	3	2,3	40, 59, 60, 79
15	Assess reliability/validity	2	3	3	2,3	39, 40, 79
16	Draw conclusions	2	3	3	2,3	39, 40

revision guides

Do**Brilliantly**

AS General Studies

Exam practice at its **best**

- **David Walton**
- **Trevor Green**
- **Series Editor: Jayne de Courcy**

Contents

Published by HarperCollins*Publishers* Ltd
77–85 Fulham Palace Road
London W6 8JB

www.**Collins**Education.com
On-line support for schools and colleges

© HarperCollins*Publishers* Ltd 2003

First published 2003

ISBN 0 00 714875 5

David Walton and Trevor Green assert the moral right to be identified as the authors of this work.

British Library Cataloguing in Publication Data
A catalogue record for this book is available from the British Library.

Edited by Jane Bryant
Production by Jack Murphy
Book design by Bob Vickers
Printed and bound in China

Acknowledgements
The Authors and Publishers are grateful to the following for permission to reproduce copyright material:
OCR pp. 37 (Q.1), 38 (Q.4), 57 (Q.2, 3 & 5), 61 (a – d), 75, 78, 81 (Q.8)
Edexcel pp. 19, 37 (Q.2 & 3), 43, 57 (Q.1), 59 (a, b, & c), 69, 73, 79 (Q.2), 81 (Q.7)
AQA pp. 9, 10, 11, 12, 15, 17, 20, 25, 26, 27, 28, 29 (Q.1 & 3), 31, 32, 33, 34, 39 (Q.1 & 2), 40 (Q.3), 41, 45, 46, 47, 48, 49, 53, 54, 55, 56, 57 (Q.4), 60, 63, 65, 71, 79 (Q.3), 80 (Q.4 & 5), 80 (Q.6)
Answers to questions taken from past examination papers are entirely the responsibility of the Authors.

Every effort has been made to contact the holders of copyright material, but if any have been inadvertently overlooked, the Publishers will be pleased to make the necessary arrangements at the first opportunity.

You might also like to visit:
www.**fire**and**water**.com
The book lover's website

What each Unit exam consists of

Below is a grid that shows at a glance what you will have to do in each of your Unit exams, depending on which specification you are studying. This grid is expanded on at the start of each section of this book (pages 8, 30 and 58).

Specification	Unit 1 Culture, Morality, Arts and Humanities	Unit 2 Science, Mathematics and Technology	Unit 3 Society, Politics and the Economy
AQA A	25 Multiple-choice comprehension + Three extended writing questions – e.g. summary; commentary; evaluation 1¼ hours	25 Multiple-choice comprehension + 25 Multiple-choice Mathematical reasoning and application of number 1¼ hours	Documentary Source Analysis Five extended writing questions (e.g. summary; commentary; evaluation, etc.) 1¼ hours
Edexcel	Four short-answer questions + Comprehension/analysis of arguments + Essay 1½ hours	Five short-answer questions + Comprehension/analysis of arguments + Essay 1¼ hours	Five short-answer questions (data response) + Comprehension/analysis of arguments + Essay 1½ hours
OCR	Comprehension Short-answer questions + Extended writing + Two-part essay 1¼ hours	Comprehension/ data analysis Two sets of short-answer questions, including evaluation of arguments + Two-part essay 1¼ hours	Comprehension/ data response Two sets of short-answer questions, including evaluation of arguments + Two-part essay 1¼ hours
AQA B	**Unit 1** (*Conflict*) Five short-answer/ mini-essay questions 1¼ hours	**Unit 2** (*Power*) Written task + Structured essay 1¼ hours	**Unit 3** (*Space*) Two data response numerical tasks/short answer questions + Extended writing/ commentary 1¼ hours

Extended writing and essay questions in General Studies

There is no fixed notion of a perfect essay in General Studies. The questions usually provide for different approaches to be adopted, certainly for different points of view, and for you to relate your own knowledge, experience and ideas to the issues involved. However,

- make sure that you **address all parts of the question**
- **use clear arguments** to explain your point of view
- **illustrate and support your arguments** by appropriate examples and references.

Where specialist knowledge is involved you should make sure that you relate this carefully to the question asked, and in terms which are understandable to 'the ordinary general reader'. Questions on science topics, for example, may require some scientific principles to be explained, as well as more general comment, and you will gain marks for doing this.

The exam boards tend to use general mark schemes based on levels which describe the overall quality of the answer being marked. **An example of such a mark scheme is given on page 21**. Your answer doesn't have to be perfect to gain full marks but everybody should aim for a mark well into the middle range.

Most, if not all, of the essay questions are expressed in several parts, and you should use these as a structure for your answer.

Always think hard and plan your answer before you start to write. Don't just start writing and see what comes out.

Do's and don't's of essay writing

- **Do** choose your topic carefully, if you have a choice.
- **Do** consider **how much** you actually have to say in answer to the question.
- **Do** organise your ideas in a **convincing sequence** to answer *each part* of the question, i.e. **Do** a plan.
- **Do** think of an **appropriate introduction** consistent with the question and your view of it – e.g. defining appropriate terms.
- **Do** support your points with **illustrations and explanations**.
- **Do** write fluently but in **short, punchy** sentences and develop only **one main point per paragraph**.
- **Do** make sure you have covered what you intended and come to a **clear conclusion**. The demands of the question should determine the structure of your answer.

- **Don't** forget the **general focus** of General Studies, so avoid a specialist answer.
- **Don't twist the question** to what you would like it to be.
- **Don't** simply write down everything you know about the topic **regardless of the question**.
- **Don't** ignore **key parts** of the question.
- **Don't forget** your plan.
- **Don't run out of time**.
- **Don't** spend **too much time** on narrative, specialist or over-technical detail, or just trying to perfect your answer.

Research has shown that the average candidate scores over **half the marks** they are going to get on a question in **a quarter of the time** they spend on it. This shows that **it is better to make a start on a new question than to spend additional time completing another**.

Assessment objectives

This shows you what knowledge, understanding and skills are being assessed in AS General Studies and their relative importance in terms of marks:

AO1 Demonstrate relevant knowledge and understanding applied to a range of issues, using skills from different disciplines (30–35%)

AO2 Communicate clearly and accurately in a concise, logical and relevant way (10–15%)

AO3 Marshal evidence and draw conclusions; select, interpret, evaluate and integrate information, data, concepts and opinions (30–35%)

AO4 Demonstrate understanding of different types of knowledge and of the relationship between them, appreciating their limitations (15–20%)

Note on AO2

This assesses the quality of your written communication, and in particular your ability to:

- select and use a form and style of writing appropriate to the question's purpose and subject matter
- organise relevant information clearly and coherently, using appropriate vocabulary
- ensure text is legible and spelling, grammar and punctuation are accurate, so that the meaning is clear.

Note on AO4

This is a new element in General Studies specifications. In the past, there has been a focus on the knowledge of facts (AO1), and the marshalling of evidence (AO3) – on what might be called 'first-order' knowledge. This is still fundamental; but AO4 is about understanding **what counts as knowledge**; about how far knowledge is based upon facts and values; and about standards of proof.

By 'different types of knowledge' we mean *different ways of getting knowledge*. We might obtain knowledge by fine measurement and calculation. This gives us a degree of **certainty**. We might obtain it by observation and by experiment. This gives us a degree of **probability**. Or we might acquire it by examination of documents and material remains or by introspection – that is, by canvassing our own experiences and feelings. This gives us a degree of **possibility**. In this sense, knowledge is a matter of degree.

Questions that are designed to test AO4 will focus on such things as:

- analysis and evaluation of the **nature of the knowledge**, evidence or arguments, for example, used in a text, set of data or other form of stimulus material;
- understanding of the crucial **differences between knowledge, belief or opinion**, and objectivity and subjectivity in arguments;
- appreciation of **what constitutes proof**, cause and effect, truth, validity, justification, and the **limits** to these;
- recognition of the **existence of personal values**, value judgements, partiality and bias in given circumstances;
- awareness of the effects upon ourselves and others of different phenomena, such as the **nature of physical, emotional and spiritual experiences**, and the ability to draw upon and analyse first-hand knowledge and understanding of these.

There are questions throughout the book on this assessment objective, and when these occur we point this out.

1 Culture, Morality, Arts and Humanities

UNIT 1 EXAMINATIONS

AQA (Specification A)

The subject area covered is *Culture, Morality, Arts and Humanities*. 50 marks are available for two sets of questions, worth 25 marks each.

- The first set is 25 **multiple-choice comprehension questions** based on a passage about 1,000 words in length.

- The second set typically consists of three questions for **short answer/extended writing** directly on the passage or on themes related to it.

- Total time allowed is $1^1/4$ hours.

- **All questions are compulsory** and you should spend approximately equal amounts of time on the two sets. Answer the multiple-choice questions first.

AQA (Specification B)

The theme of this paper is *Conflict*. 60 marks are available for five extended writing/mini-essay questions worth 12 marks each.

- There is **one** question on **each of the five subject areas** for the specification: *Arts and Media, Beliefs and Values, Industry and Commerce, Science and Technology, Society and Politics*; and **all are compulsory**.

- Time allowed is $1^1/4$ hours.

- **You should write at least a substantial paragraph on each question**.

Edexcel

The subject area covered is *Aspects of Culture (Culture, Morality, Arts and Humanities)*. 50 marks are available for three sets of questions.

- Section A consists of four **compulsory short-answer questions** worth 4 or 5 marks each on key topics for this part of the specification.

- Section B is based on a passage of about 650 words and has three **compulsory short-answer comprehension questions** worth between 2 and 4 marks each, plus 3 marks for overall quality of written communication.

- In Section C you choose to answer one from three **essay questions on key topics**. It is worth 20 marks.

- Total time allowed is $1^1/2$ hours.

OCR

The subject area covered is *The Cultural Domain (Culture, Morality, Arts and Humanities)*. 100 marks are available for three sets of questions.

- The first question in Section A consists of a number of **compulsory short-answer comprehension questions** worth 25 marks all together, based on one or two passages of about 600 words in total length.

- The second question is a **compulsory piece of extended writing** based on a theme related to the passage(s) and is also worth 25 marks.

- In Section B you choose to answer one from three **two-part essay questions on key topics** for the unit. It is worth 50 marks. The first part requires you to define or explain a concept for 10 marks and the second to discuss aspects of it for 40 marks.

- Total time allowed is $1^1/4$ hours.

Read the passage below and answer the questions that follow.

THE ELECTRONIC MEDIA

(1) In California there is a group called the 'Couch Potatoes', who consider themselves 'the true televisionaries'. They take their name from their favourite place for vegetating in front of the TV set, and from a vegetable with many eyes. An advertisement to recruit members for the group goes like this: 'Do you enjoy excessive amounts of TV viewing? Were some of the most enjoyable times of your life experienced in front of your TV set? Were your formative years nurtured by the 'electronic babysitter'? Are you annoyed by cry-baby intellectuals who claim that TV viewing is counterproductive and a waste of time? Like to do most of your living on the couch?'

(2) Asked by a reporter to comment on a two-way cable system that allows viewers to talk back to the television, one of the 'Couch Potatoes' responded: 'Why watch TV if you have to think and respond? As far as I'm concerned, the main point of watching TV is that it lets you avoid having to do that. To put it another way, if you're going to have to respond to your TV you might as well go out and cultivate friendships or read a book or something.'

(3) The 'Couch Potatoes' consciously caricature, by carrying to an absurd extreme, the idea that television is a passive anti-intellectual medium, a medium that encourages people to vegetate. This opinion is shared by many others who consider the dangers of television too serious to make fun of. Falling scores on national tests, rising levels of violence in society, students' inability to write well – these and other trends are blamed on the long hours recent generations of children have spent watching television.

(4) In the past few years a new medium has come along to fascinate young people and worry their elders: video games. Some adults fear that, even more than television, the games are at best frivolous and at worst mindless, numbing, and violent. While many see the popularity of microcomputers among the young as a promising trend, others fear that they reinforce asocial or even antisocial tendencies.

(5) My own opinion is that the damaging effects which the electronic media can have on children are not intrinsic to the media but grow out of the ways in which the media are used. Much of the content of commercial TV shows may have a negative effect on children's social attitudes. Commercials themselves use sophisticated techniques to manipulate viewers into wanting certain products and young children have no defences against such techniques. In addition television watching can become a passive, deadening activity, if adults do not guide their children's viewing and teach them to watch critically and to learn from what they watch.

(6) But television and the newer electronic media, if used wisely, have great positive potential for learning and development. They give children different mental skills from those developed by reading and writing. Television is a better medium than the printed word for conveying certain types of information and it makes learning available to groups of children who do not do well in traditional school situations – and even to people who cannot read. Video games introduce children to the world of microcomputers at a time when computers are becoming increasingly important both in many jobs and in daily life. The interactive quality of both video games and computers forces children actively to create stimuli and information, not merely consume them.

(7) The idea that television can be a positive force in children's lives has been around for decades. A classic study was done in England in the 1950s, when less than 10 percent of English families had TV sets and it was still possible to compare children who had television with children who did not. The authors suggested that parents and teachers inform themselves about television, not just to prevent children from seeing harmful programmes, but to encourage them to watch worthwhile ones. They recommended discussing programmes at home and in school, both to counteract one-sided views and to reinforce the impact of good programmes. They also recommended teaching children critical viewing skills that would help them, for example, to distinguish fantasy from reality.

**Adapted from the introduction to *Mind and Media*
by Patricia Marks Greenfield**

Question types 1 and 4

Each of the questions carries 1 mark.

Read the passage entitled **THE ELECTRONIC MEDIA** and answer the questions asked or implied by choosing the answer represented by the letter **A–D** which you think best.

1. According to paragraphs 1 and 2 the 'Couch Potatoes' believe that television is the best form of

    A   escapism.

    B   stimulation.

    C   education.

    D   nurture.

2. The 'Couch Potatoes' advertisement and their approach to television viewing in paragraphs 1 and 2 is described by the author in a manner which is

    A   'deadly serious'.

    B   'off the point'.

    C   'holier than thou'.

    D   'tongue in cheek'.

3. According to the author in the third paragraph, the 'Couch Potatoes'

    A   believe that children watch too much television.

    B   blame television for many recent social problems.

    C   deliberately exaggerate the negative effects of television.

    D   support those who criticise television.

4. The word 'caricature' is used in paragraph 3 as

    A   a noun.

    B   an adjective.

    C   an adverb.

    D   a verb.

5. The difference between 'asocial' and 'antisocial' as used in paragraph 4 is

    A   putting your interests before other people's as opposed to theirs before yours.

    B   ignoring society as opposed to acting against it.

    C   reacting violently towards others as opposed to merely negatively.

    D   doing nothing for society as opposed to doing something.

6. In paragraphs 3 and 4 a number of criticisms are made of TV and video games, the least serious of which is that they

   A   are a waste of time.

   B   affect academic performance.

   C   undermine the development of social skills.

   D   encourage violence.

7. When the author states in paragraph 5 that 'the damaging effects which the electronic media can have on children are not *intrinsic* to the media', she means that they are not

   A   damaging to the media.

   B   necessarily harmful to children.

   C   caused by the media themselves.

   D   the result of the programmes, but of the advertisements.

8. Which of the following observations does the author make in paragraph 6 in support of the use of electronic media in education?

   1   Television can replace books.

   2   Children are introduced to computers.

   3   Learning is often interactive.

   4   Children learn more quickly.

   5   Electronic media encourage an active approach to learning.

   Answer
   A   if **1**, **2** and **4** only are correct.
   B   if **1**, **3** and **5** only are correct.
   C   if **2**, **3** and **5** only are correct.
   D   if **2**, **4** and **5** only are correct.

9. According to the researchers, parents can 'counteract one-sided views' (paragraph 7) by

   A   choosing the right programmes for children to watch.

   B   encouraging children to talk about programmes they have watched.

   C   restricting the amount of television that children watch.

   D   role playing programmes that children have watched.

10. Each of the following was a recommendation of the 1950s study referred to in paragraph 7 **except**

   A   parents should discuss television with their children.

   B   parents should limit the amount of television watched by children.

   C   parents should be more aware of what is being shown on television.

   D   parents should encourage children to be more selective about what they watch.

Question	Correct answer	Examiner's hints
1.	A	This first question **tests your understanding of the overall sense** of the first two paragraphs. The 'Couch Potatoes' see TV as a passive, anti-intellectual medium, so this rules out Options B, C and D, which are all too positive. The correct answer is A: 'escapism'.
2.	D	This question **tests your appreciation of the tone** of the introduction. The 'Couch Potatoes' approach is deliberately exaggerated, humorous and ironic – it is 'tongue in cheek' (not entirely serious).
3.	C	What is the purpose of the reference to the 'Couch Potatoes'? **The answer is in the first sentence of paragraph 3.** The negative aspects of TV are being stressed all the time and are being exaggerated for deliberate effect.
4.	D	**'Caricature' can be used as a noun or a verb.** A caricature (noun) is a deliberately exaggerated description, but *to* caricature (verb) means to describe or imitate in a deliberately exaggerated manner. In paragraph 3 'The 'Couch Potatoes' consciously caricature …' It's what they are doing, so is a verb.
5.	B	**You should understand the different meanings of prefixes and how they alter the sense of words.** 'a-' means without or lacking – e.g. 'amoral' means without morals. 'anti-' means opposed to or against – e.g. anti-freeze or antipathy. Option B is the only one which fits exactly – ignoring society ('asocial') rather than acting against it ('antisocial').
6.	A	Here you have to **evaluate a series of points** made in paragraphs 3 and 4 and assess them in order of their significance according to the author. **The clue lies in the author's use of 'at best' in paragraph 4.** Of all the criticisms of TV and video games (they adversely affect school performance, undermine children's social development, encourage violence, etc.) 'at best frivolous' (meaning a waste of time) has to be the least serious.
7.	C	**This is simply a question of what 'intrinsic' means** (belonging to something by its very nature). In this case 'not *intrinsic* to the media' means not caused by the media themselves.
8.	C	This is a multi-part question. **Which of the five points in support of the electronic media is the author making in paragraph 6?** They introduce children to computers (2), learning is often interactive (3) and they can encourage an active approach to learning (5). The author does not claim that they can replace books (1) or that children learn more quickly (4), so the answer has to be C.
9.	B	With multiple-choice questions you often have to decide which is the **most appropriate and precise answer in the context.** All the answers given here are possible, but the paragraph does not mention role play – which rules out D. The other options are all suggested in the passage, but A (choosing the right programmes) is too general, and C (restricting the amount watched) would not necessarily produce the required result. Enabling children to develop more rounded opinions (i.e. parents encouraging their children to talk about programmes) is specifically designed to 'counteract one-sided views', so the answer is B.
10.	B	Here you have to **identify which statement does not fit.** As always, **be careful and very precise.** All the options could apply to the passage as a whole, but limiting the amount of television children watch does *not* relate to the 1950s study.

When tackling multiple choice questions, always follow this procedure:

- **Step 1 – scan all the material relating to the test as a whole**, including the questions, to give you a quick idea of what the content is about.
- **Step 2 – read through the stimulus material carefully and establish what the text is covering**. At this stage you should be focusing on the key points and the main thread of the arguments. Underline what you think are the key points or main topic sentence(s) in each section as you go. Most often this will the first sentence of each paragraph.
- **Step 3 – work through each of the questions in turn**. Think through your answer before you choose the response you think is correct.

Speed and decisiveness are essential. Multiple-choice tests are designed to cover a lot of ground in a short period of time. The questions are worth the same marks (1 only) whether they are easy or difficult. In the AQA test you have about 35 minutes to complete this part of the test, so you should spend the first 7 minutes or so on Steps 1 and 2. You then have approximately 1 minute to spend on each of the 25 questions – and 3 minutes to **review your answers** at the end.

Concentrate hard but briefly on the question in hand. If it points you to a particular part of the passage, this is where the answer will be. Do not be distracted by the questions you have passed over or have not yet done. Do not panic. Some of the questions are designed to be beyond all but the best candidates. Be decisive, and **try not to change your mind**. If you are unsure, go with the answer you first thought was right.

Return to the more difficult items at the end and try to **eliminate the less likely alternatives**. Use your deductive powers to reduce the element of guesswork.

Answer all the questions. Marks are not deducted for incorrect answers, so you have nothing to lose in the last resort by guessing.

Do not expect to get all the questions right – 65–70% will get you a Grade A. Pass quickly over questions that you have no idea about, and **concentrate on the ones you feel you ought to be able to get right**.

For Questions 1, 2, 3 and 5 refer to the passage **THE ELECTRONIC MEDIA** on pages 9–10.
The questions should be answered using continuous prose.

Question 1 (question type 5)

Using the author's examples and ideas, as well as any of your own, outline what you
think are **(a)** the weaknesses and **(b)** the strengths of the electronic media for children's
learning and development.   [8 marks]

ALEX'S ANSWER

The author suggests that the electronic media is 'mindnumbing' and makes children
'passive'. I think that this is because it is not interactive or challenging enough to
stimulate active learning. If the television programmes and computer games played have a
more educational theme and challenge them into using some cognitive processes it could be
beneficial. I think that media such as television and computers make children antisocial
which may hinder them as they are not interacting with other children. It may benefit
learning because it could make learning more enjoyable and therefore children will be
more willing to actively participate in educational activities.

5/8

EMILY'S ANSWER

One of the principal weaknesses of the electronic media for children's learning and
development is that in many respects passivity is encouraged so that children lose the
opportunity for active participation and mental effort. Similarly the media cannot be
thought of as a substitute for books since literacy is crucial in today's society and the
skills of reading and writing must not be neglected. There is an additional danger in the
addictive nature of the media, which, if not kept under control, could turn the activity
into a passive and numbing experience, which would hold children back in their learning
and development.

However, there are also a number of strengths in the electronic media. The first of
these is that if the media are used wisely and constructively, then there is much
potential for learning and development. Television can offer children different mental skills
which cannot be obtained from books, particularly for those children who cannot read.
Video games, though they are considered by many to be mindless and violent, are
interactive and introduce children to the world of microcomputers, a vital aspect of our
modern technological society.

7/8

How to score full marks

Alex's answer is a reasonable one. He **summarises a number of key points** quite well.

However, the question asks you to **outline** the weaknesses and strengths and **Alex's summary is too brief and too general** on both aspects. He has not included details from the text, such as the references to:

- addictive and violent material
- the need for variety and selection (critical viewing)
- the continuing importance of literacy
- the strength of the visual aspects of the media compared with print
- the value of access to modern technology.

Emily's answer is **more developed in terms of structure and detail**. She deals with the weaknesses and strengths in **separate paragraphs**. The points she has detailed **stand out more clearly**; there are **more of them** and they are mostly **better supported or explained**.

The main reason why Emily did not score full marks is that she did not attempt to clarify what the 'different mental skills' referred to in the second paragraph might be and **just quoted this directly from the passage**. As the test rubric states, **using your own words to show your understanding is a key requirement**.

Don't forget ...

When you are asked to outline (or summarise) points made in the passage, **assemble the points or arguments for or against a case** (or both as in the question above) in the form of strengths and weaknesses.

You can introduce your own ideas, but you do not have to unless the question asks you to. It may be best to concentrate on extracting all the main points from the passage relevant to the question as succinctly as you can.

Do not just copy from the text. Use your own words where appropriate. The examiner needs to know whether you understand fully what you have written and your own words will show this better.

Don't over-elaborate if all you need to do is compile a list of points.

Question 2 (question types 6, 7)

What do you understand by the phrase 'critical viewing skills', referred to in paragraph 7?

What steps can parents and teachers take to ensure the development of these skills?

In your answer you may wish to discuss such activities as watching television, playing computer games and using the Internet.

[8 marks]

ALEX'S ANSWER

Critical viewing skills mean to me that the person viewing will have the ability to fully understand what they are watching. They can understand any underlying message or theme that the programme has. They would be able to analyse and evaluate the information presented and make objective decisions about what they are viewing.

Ultimately they will be able to appreciate the artistic element of the acting, for example, thus making the activity less 'mindnumbing' and 'passive', as the viewer is actively participating in what they are seeing. Critical viewing is essentially the ability to appreciate what you are watching for its true worth and being able to distinguish between worthwhile programmes and those which are a waste of time.

4/8

How to score full marks

Alex's answer to the first part of this two-part question is excellent, but he has completely ignored the second – equally important and probably more straightforward – part. **Always make sure you address all parts of the question**.

Alex needed to go on to discuss the steps that parents and teachers can take to ensure the development of critical viewing skills. These could include:
- carefully choosing material for children to watch and restricting access to unsuitable channels, videos and websites
- shared viewing and encouraging discussion of programmes, games and use of the Internet
- agreements on what is good and useful material, how much and when
- enabling children to form their own judgements and develop their own preferences in an informed way
- making effective use of different media in well constructed learning programmes.

Always **make use of any prompts you are given in the question**, which is something Alex did not do. The suggestions that you consider '… television, … computer games and … the Internet', as well as the roles of 'parents and teachers', are there to imply that these may be related but different activities.

Draw on your own ideas and experience. Illustrations and examples are often useful for clarifying points, particularly if they stem from your own experience.

Don't forget ...

Answer each question as it is asked. This seems obvious, but often students get carried away and forget some vital part.

Answer each part of the question. Use the structure of the question to help you do this.

If the question suggests you might **consider particular aspects**, make sure you do.

Question 3 (question types 9, 10)

Identify different types of knowledge or argument used in the passage and discuss how effectively they are used.

[5 marks]

TOM'S ANSWER

In the passage the author discusses the effects of the electronic media on children. The early part of the passage concentrates on concerns about the negative effects of television and video games. In the second part of the passage the author gives his or her opinion that television can be a positive force in children's lives. The author's overall argument seems to be that the media can have good and bad effects and that it all depends on how they are used. This is effective because the author presents arguments on both sides before coming to a conclusion.

(3/5)

How to score full marks

- Although Tom's answer is quite clear and coherent, **it is too brief and he does not develop the points he makes**. In this question, two marks are allocated to each of two developed points about the nature of the knowledge or arguments in the passage and a final mark is given for comments about how they are used by the author.

- **On the negative side of the argument**, to score two marks instead of just one Tom would have needed to go on to say that the author is reporting mostly generalised opinions of other people, e.g. 'Some people fear that, even more than television, the games are at best frivolous, and at worst mindless, numbing and violent'.

- **On the positive side of the argument**, to score the second mark, Tom could have added that the author quotes a study done in England in the 1950s. This is presented as authoritative (argument by authority). Although the results of the study are not given in detail, it is possible to deduce from the recommendations that television and video games can be used to good effect, provided that parents and children adopt an active and critical approach to viewing, rather than just letting the children watch whatever and as much as they want.

- **Tom's final points are well expressed**.

Don't forget ...

Even questions worth only a few marks may require analysis and evaluation.

You can expect to see questions on **the nature of the knowledge, arguments or evidence used in the passage** in most AS General Studies examinations. This is Assessment Objective 4 (demonstrate understanding of different types of knowledge and of the relationship between them, appreciating their limitations) and accounts for 15–20% of the overall assessment.

You need to show understanding of:
- the **crucial differences** between such things as knowledge, belief, opinion, objectivity and subjectivity in arguments
- **what constitutes proof**
- **cause and effect**
- **what we mean by truth, validity, justification**
- **what represents a value judgement, partiality and bias**.

See pages 21 and 24 for more on this.

Question 4 (question types 2, 7)

Outline what is meant by religious experience, using an example. [5 marks]

NAOMI'S ANSWER

To me religious experience is when I feel I am close to God, such as when I go to Church to take Communion. The Communion service consists of readings from the Bible, hymns and prayers to celebrate the life and goodness of Christ, who Christians believe is the Son of God and who died on the cross to save us. We pray to God to bring goodness into our lives and save us from sinning, so that when we die we can be re-united with our loved ones and enjoy ever-lasting life in Heaven.

5/5

How to score full marks

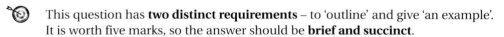

- This question has **two distinct requirements** – to 'outline' and give 'an example'. It is worth five marks, so the answer should be **brief and succinct**.

- Naomi does **exactly what the question asks** in both respects. She describes what is a religious experience for her by means of a **valid example** which is **well described and explained**. She could have described religious experience in a more general way, e.g. when someone undergoes a conversion, or experiences a vision or some kind of miraculous event, which is how people often describe a religious experience.

- **Drawing directly on your own personal experience** is often very effective. It makes what you say 'real' – and it works extremely well here.

EXTENDED WRITING QUESTIONS

Question 5 (question types 3, 8, 10, 11)

'Falling scores on national tests, rising levels of violence in society, students' inability to write well – these and other trends are blamed on the long hours recent generations of children have spent watching television.' (paragraph 3)

To what extent is it valid to say that television and the electronic media generally have created the problems outlined above?   [9 marks]

Good – a well-considered start. The use of such phrases as 'could be argued' and 'considered by many' is appropriate to this kind of question and suggests a degree of detachment from the rather sweeping quotation, but it doesn't rule out the possibility and explains why at the end of the first paragraph. This shows mature judgement and evaluation.

Good development. Picks up other aspects of the quotation and comments on them in similar fashion.

An important point and well put, but left as a general statement. Emily could improve this middle section by more development and clarification, perhaps giving some examples of how the media can have positive benefits rather than negative influences. There is also just a suggestion of 'padding' in the repetition.

A valid and well expressed conclusion, but too general. She ought at least to give some examples of other possible causes for the problems of violence, poor educational performance and standards of literacy.

EMILY'S ANSWER

It could be argued that the electronic media have contributed to the problems outlined here. Indeed, the dangers of video games are considered by many to include the violent images which are frequently depicted, and which perhaps influence children to act in a violent manner copying what they have seen and 'taken part in'.

Television, similarly, could be said to portray not only violent images, but also to encourage passivity and mindlessness in children, which could lead to falling scores in national tests. Also the increase in television-watching and the decrease in reading is a significant problem, since although television and computer games could be argued to introduce other skills in children, literacy remains crucial to the education of our society and needs to be promoted.

However, perhaps it should be noted that the problems of society cannot be blamed entirely on the electronic media. Certainly not all children fall instantly under the influence of the television or computer games and indeed, as has already been mentioned, certain aspects of the electronic media are extremely beneficial to the development of children's minds and skills.

There is no one thing on which all the problems of today's society can be blamed. Perhaps there is an element of truth in that television and the electronic media in general are contributing factors to the problems; however, such sweeping generalisations should not be made, as the media can also clearly be seen to have a number of strengths as well as disadvantages.

(6/9)

20

How to score full marks

 Emily's answer gives an overall impression of a **good general commentary showing balance and mature judgement**. It gained a top Level 2 mark (see below). For a high Level 3 mark she needed to **go beyond the general statements and into more detail** – about, for example:

- **other possible causes**, such as violence in the home, boredom from unemployment.

- **the nature of the evidence and support/proof** for such claims. For example, scores on national tests are in theory verifiable by looking at results of SATs, GCSEs and A levels.

- **the problem of establishing whether such trends are real**, and – more importantly – the even greater problem of **demonstrating a direct cause and effect**. It is very difficult to separate out one potential cause (variable) from another and prove any links (direct or even indirect). What may apply in some cases may not apply generally. For instance, very few people who watch violent videos or plays violent computer games turn out to be violent.

 An important dimension to this type of question requires a **more abstract discussion** of the nature of the problem and how arguments may be justified or not.

Don't forget ...

This type of question requires you to **evaluate statements of opinion and how far they can be backed up with evidence**.

To answer the question fully you need to give a more theoretical discussion of **the nature of the problem and how arguments may be justified or not**.

Be prepared to challenge the question or the values and assumptions within it, if appropriate – or at least ask yourself how certain you think your (or anybody else's) knowledge can be in such circumstances. Some issues may be more to do with opinion and belief than with empirical evidence that can be put to the test.

See page 24 for more on this.

Typical mark scheme for General Studies

Level of response	Range of marks available	Criteria and descriptors: knowledge, understanding, argument, evaluation, communication
Level 3	Above 65%	Approaching a comprehensive response demonstrating good grasp of the nature and range of issues; knowledge and understanding of key principles and evidence; interprets and illustrates arguments coherently and convincingly with fluency.
Level 2	36–65%	Reasonably competent attempt, with reasonable grasp of the issues; some understanding and appreciation of the key principles; moderate range of argument and exemplification, expressed with reasonable clarity and accuracy.
Level 1	Up to 35%	Limited response showing uncertain grasp, knowledge and understanding; lack of clarity and appropriate exemplification; weak expression.
Level 0	0%	No response or relevant points.

The examiners are looking for a range of criteria, which balance precise appreciation of the demands of the question and related issues, knowledge and understanding of the topic, a range of supporting argument and illustration, clear and accurate expression. You should aim to do enough on all of these fronts to get comfortably into Level 2. If all your answers are at the top Level 2 mark, you will probably gain an A grade.

FREE-STANDING ESSAY QUESTIONS

Question 6 (question types 3, 7, 8, 9, 10, 11)

What do you understand by the term 'morality'?   [10 marks]

Some people claim there are moral rules which should never be disobeyed.
How far do you think such a claim is justified?   [40 marks]

This is a rather simple explanation of what 'morality' is, written from a personal standpoint. It contains valid points and elements that could have been developed further.

This section is far too simple and tries to deal with very complex issues in a sweeping way. It raises many more questions than it answers. What kind of punishment and who should carry it out, for example? What about killing in self-defence or in warfare? Occasionally there are genuine moral dilemmas, where it may take a questionable act to prevent greater wrong-doing.

This is a circular argument. It is sincere and seems watertight, but is too superficial to address real-life issues.

MARY'S ANSWER

What I understand by morality is that it is about always doing good things and thinking good things. Some people I know are more 'moral' than others, which generally means that they are more thoughtful about other people and less selfish in their behaviour. I always try to behave morally as my parents have always taught me the difference between right and wrong. I know that they would be upset if I did something wrong and I would never try to do anything which would hurt them.

6/10

I think that there are some moral rules which should never be disobeyed. The 10 Commandments tell us 'Thou shalt not steal' and 'Thou shalt not commit murder' and it is against the law to do these things. God tells us what is right and wrong in the Bible and I believe we should always try to do what is right, so I would never commit murder and I have never stolen anything. I am a pacifist and a vegetarian, so I believe that all killing of people and animals is wrong. People who do these things should be punished and made to pay for their crimes, like the people who deliberately flew those planes into the Twin Towers on the 11 September 2001. They should be caught and punished for the terrible crimes that they committed. What they did was totally wrong and this is a good example of a moral rule which should never be disobeyed.

In fact I do not think that there are any moral rules which should be disobeyed, otherwise they would not be moral rules. I think all moral rules should be obeyed and that is why they are called moral.

10/40

22

How to score full marks

- Mary's answer does not score very highly, because **it fails to recognise its own limitations**. Her response is **too brief and superficial**. She **does not recognise the complexity of the issues**. Mary starts off quite well, but later she seems to be **unaware of the implications of what she is saying**.

- Mary's **definition is reasonable** and she is right about the 10 Commandments laying down rules – almost all religions argue that it is God who decides what is right and wrong and this is set out in religious books like the Christian Bible and Muslim Qur'an. She is also entitled to state her position as a pacifist and vegetarian. There is no doubt also that the 11 September crimes were terrible and justify a response of some kind, but at this point she **'ducks' the responsibility** on punishment – and does she believe that all soldiers or those who work in abattoirs are immoral?

- **The questions require more than the assertion of a personal position.** Like a lot of questions in General Studies, they require more awareness of the possible positions of others – **a more objective viewpoint**.

- You don't have to be religious to behave morally either and there are **many different theories** on what makes an action right or wrong. Many people take the view that **the intended consequences of an action** are what make it right or wrong. If you have a choice, you should choose the action which will produce the greatest benefit or the least suffering for those who will be affected. This is known as **Utilitarianism**. For any society to exist without conflict there needs to be a sense of '**shared values**' where we broadly know how people are likely to act and where personal self-interest is balanced against the interests of others. These values form part of an accepted **moral code**; some are enshrined in law and others are a matter of personal behaviour and they are influenced by, and acquired through, those with whom we have daily contact – family, friends, school, neighbourhood.

A moral decision to be made . . .

Exam technique – points to remember

Knowledge is gained in different ways, for example:

- by precise **measurement and calculation** (which gives a degree of certainty)
- by **observation and experiment** (gives a degree of probability)
- by **examination** of documents, artefacts, ideas, thoughts and feelings (gives a degree of possibility).

Some knowledge can be accepted as fairly certain. For example, when we are considering the behaviour of **things (phenomena)**, the **evidence** could be described as **hard or objective** and we can speak about **facts, laws and proof**. When we are considering beings, particularly **people**, the evidence is **softer/more subjective. In the natural and social sciences we tend to talk about theories rather than laws**.

In the humanities and arts the evidence is softer still, although we can still be 'scientific'/disciplined/objective in how we go about assembling it. Historians, for example, work on facts (what happened), but they also have to select and interpret to make sense of them. In doing this they make judgements and express opinions. If people ignore some of the evidence they could be accused of being biased or partial. If they dismiss some of the evidence as not relevant, we may accept their opinion as valid if we agree with their argument or justification.

Mark allocation for short-answer questions:

- For all short-answer questions, **consider the number of marks allocated**. This will give you an idea of how much detail (in the form of specific points) you should go into and how much development (supporting arguments and examples) you need to give.
- A question worth one mark may require only a single word, phrase or sentence and no development; one worth two marks may ask for a definition and an example (one mark for each).
- Questions worth 5 marks or more will require more extended writing – a paragraph at least, if the question requires continuous writing, at least five distinct points if bullet points are allowed. **The more marks there are, the more you will be expected to write**, and in some cases your answer will become more of a mini-essay.

Questions that begin with 'How far do you think …?' or 'To what extent…?' are very common in General Studies. They generally require a **balanced consideration of complex problems** that often have no single answer and **awareness that there are a number of legitimate viewpoints** that can be argued depending on the circumstances. Give your opinion, but **show your awareness of, and examine, a number of possible views before committing yourself to a single position, if required**.

Where the evidence cannot be certain we may draw upon belief. Often we believe in a set of values, things that we regard as right or wrong, good or bad, or simply 'true'. Beliefs and values may have more to do with how we feel about something than facts, or with things that cannot be proved, although they may also be based on conclusions we have reached from our own and others' experiences.

Read the passage below and answer the questions that follow.

THE COMEDIAN'S CULTURE CONUNDRUM

(1) Jokes about race have finally been given an official stamp of approval. The Broadcasting Standards Commission (BSC) has stuck its head above the parapet to say it is fine for comedians to poke fun at religious and cultural differences – provided they are talking about their own faith. The new guideline, in a recent BSC report prepared by an academic, really only serves to codify what performers on the alternative comedy circuit have known for years – you can get away with religious, xenophobic* and, in some cases, downright racist material, provided you appear to be telling it against yourself.

(2) But is this state of affairs really so desirable? Just because predominantly white and middle-class audiences laugh at comics from ethnic minorities who are taking the rise out of their parents and communities, does that make it harmless? The BBC's *Goodness Gracious Me* has made a name for itself sending up the team's ethnic origins. But it would have been wonderful if they had employed their undoubted comedy talents without constantly playing the racial stereotype card. Similarly, TV star Lenny Henry spent his formative years in showbiz as Britain's best-known 'black hack' – a comedian who runs down the tramlines of black/white humour. It is only in recent years that he has transcended that level to become a comic who is secure enough not to base his comedy on his skin colour.

(3) Recently, I watched a talented young black comic storm a show with a routine about the alleged sexual promiscuity and general uncouthness of American rap stars. Afterwards, a working-class white comedian who was in the audience at the club in London's Crouch End told me that he had found the routine 'offensive and racist'. He explained his reaction by saying the audience had assumed that the performer was taking the mickey out of his own people, when in fact he was a Cambridge University-educated man – culturally far-removed from the American ghetto rappers he was crucifying.

(4) To many comedy fans, black is black. They fail to make the distinction between performers of African or West Indian origin, allowing black comedians to send up cultural backgrounds different from their own. It begs the question: is a Nigerian comic who ridicules Jamaican Rastafarians in a xenophobic fashion truly on sounder ground than a white comedian who does the same?

(5) Anglo-Iranian comedienne Shappi Khorsandi says jokes about racial differences are fine – if you know where to draw the line. She has cut a section of her act – about how Iranian men dance – because she felt it was a gratuitous send-up. And after doing a recent spot at the Comedy Store in London, she said another performer objected to a

'racist' Irish joke she had cracked: 'Irish boy bands are all very well, but who's going to mend the roads?' 'He said I might as well be Bernard Manning with a gag like that,' says Khorsandi. 'He was absolutely right. I spend my whole act going on about what people think about me (being Iranian), and then do an Irish joke.'

(6) Leading comedy agent Paul Duddridge says he hates the white chattering classes setting the agenda on what is permissible in comedy. He has discouraged his black acts from writing material to please '*Guardian* readers or writers'. Duddridge does not want them to 'positively stereotype' black culture, never saying anything bad about it whilst running down white people.

(7) And he would also like to see white acts doing ruthlessly honest material about other races. 'It's racist not to,' says Duddridge, 'with the racism being that white people think they are so powerful that the minute they mention something seemingly negative about another culture, it is somehow going to destroy it. Duddridge is against rules on racial comedy. He believes the new BSC guidelines are wholly unnecessary and calls for more comedians to be courageous, as Channel 5 star Jerry Sadowitz and the BBC's Jim Davidson have been in writing material in an area that is, to many, taboo.

(8) What is really peculiar about xenophobic comedy is that it is open season on some nationalities but not others. No one questions the probity of attacking Australians or Americans. But if the Americans or Australians in question were black, comics would not dare to do the same routines about them.

(9) 'Ricky Grover, who is one of my acts, will go and do gigs for black audiences whilst wearing a big, stupid Afro wig,' adds Duddridge, with evident pride. 'He's the only white comic I know with the bottle to do that. I believe 100 per cent that you can say anything if you do it in the right way. It's all contextual.'

(10) If done with irony, there is room for racial stereotyping gags on television and in the clubs. And it would certainly be good to see comedians of all races and creeds exploring the area more bravely. But codifying who can tell what sort of joke sets a dangerous precedent. In the real world, every gag and every punchline should be judged on its merits. The relationship between race and comedy is a far more complex business than any TV watchdog's guidelines can satisfactorily encompass.

* xenophobia = fear or hatred of foreigners

Adapted from *The comedian's culture conundrum*
by Ollie Wilson from *The Stage*, June 1999

Question types 1, 4

Each of the questions carries 1 mark.

Read the passage entitled **THE COMEDIAN'S CULTURE CONUNDRUM** and answer the questions asked or implied by choosing the answer represented by the letter **A–D** which you think best.

1. When the author says that 'The Broadcasting Standards Commission (BSC) has stuck its head above the parapet . . .' (paragraph 1), he means that the Commission has
    A made a serious error of judgement.
    B indicated its position on a controversial issue.
    C stepped out of line with the general view on the subject.
    D shown where the limits of common sense lie.

2. 'To stick your head above the parapet' (paragraph 1) is a figurative expression taken from
    A mythology.
    B politics.
    C the theatre.
    D warfare.

3. The main point which the author is seeking to make in paragraph 3 is that
    A race is about culture and class, as well as skin colour.
    B the comedian obviously hated American rappers.
    C what black people find funny, white people can find offensive, and vice versa.
    D sometimes audiences do not understand what they are laughing at.

4. In paragraph 4 the author's tone is
    A approving.
    B disapproving.
    C neutral.
    D uncertain.

5. 'It's all contextual' (paragraph 9) could also be expressed as 'it all depends on the
    A comedian'.
    B joke'.
    C race'.
    D situation'.

6. 'With irony' as used by the author in paragraph 10 means
    A not intending seriously what you say.
    B showing clearly what you think.
    C being brave enough not to hold back.
    D in a cautious and controlled way.

For **Question 7** answer

A   if both statement X and statement Y are true and Y is a correct explanation of X.

B   if both statements are true but Y is not a correct explanation of X.

C   if statement X is true and statement Y is false.

D   if both statements are false.

	Statement X		*Statement Y*
7.	Comedians like Jim Davidson (paragraph 7) have been working with material that is, to many, taboo	BECAUSE	every joke needs to be judged on its own merits.

8. In this passage the author's objections to the BSC guideline include which of the following?

   1   It takes insufficient account of differences within ethnic groups.

   2   It oversimplifies the relationship between race and comedy.

   3   Jokes against one's own culture are not necessarily harmless.

   Answer
   A   if **1** only is correct.
   B   if **1** and **2** only are correct.
   C   if **2** and **3** only are correct.
   D   if all of them are correct.

9. 'The comedian's culture conundrum' in the title of the passage is that

   A   comedians should not be restricted in the material they choose.

   B   the television regulator has made racist jokes acceptable.

   C   comedians face a complex problem in deciding what is acceptable.

   D   all comedians are limited by their own cultural background.

10. A crucial weakness of the passage is that

   A   it does not contain enough examples of racist jokes which may offend.

   B   it fails to define clearly the difference between acceptable and unacceptable racial humour.

   C   there are not enough comedians prepared to test out the author's theory.

   D   it is not always possible to appreciate the merits of racist comedy.

Answers can be found on pages 82–83.

Refer to the passage **THE COMEDIAN'S CULTURE CONUNDRUM** where appropriate.

Question types 5, 6

1. Using examples and ideas from the passage, as well as any of your own if you wish, outline the difficulties comedians and audiences may face in dealing with humour about race. [8 marks]

Question types 9, 10, 11

2. 'You can say anything if you do it in the right way. It's all contextual.'

   Comment on both the strength and weakness of this argument by the author about comedy and race. [6 marks]

Question types 3, 7, 8, 9

3. Why is comedy such a popular form of entertainment?

   In your response you may wish to consider such factors as the nature of comedy, the range of different types of comedy available (on radio, television, film, in the theatre and in clubs), as well as the different forms of experience they provide and their particular appeal for specific audiences. You may refer to examples offered in the passage or draw on others from your own experience. [20 marks]

Question types 3, 7, 8, 9, 10, 11

4. 'We live in a free society; therefore there should be no censorship.' To what extent do you consider this to be a valid argument? [10 marks]

   What limits and controls do you think should apply to public performances, displays or published material? Give reasons to support your arguments. [40 marks]

Answers can be found on pages 83–87.

UNIT 2 EXAMINATIONS

AQA (Specification A)

The subject area covered is *Science, Mathematics and Technology*. 50 marks are available for two sets of multiple-choice questions, worth 25 marks each.

- The first set is 25 science **comprehension questions** based on a passage about 600 words in length, graphs, charts and other figures.

- The second set is 25 questions on **mathematical reasoning and applications**.

- Total time allowed is $1^1/4$ hours.

- **All questions are compulsory** and you are advised to spend approximately equal amounts of time on the two sets.

AQA (Specification B)

The theme of this paper is *Power* and questions are drawn from the five major subject areas of *Arts and Media, Beliefs and Values, Industry and Commerce, Science and Technology, Society and Politics*. A maximum of 70 marks are available for two pieces of structured writing.

- Section A is a **compulsory scenario** of about 500 words to which you are have to respond by writing a letter, report, transcript of a discussion, etc. on the issues following a given format. It is worth 40 marks.

- Section B is a choice of **one from two essays** worth 30 marks on key topics for this part of the specification.

- Total time allowed is $1^1/4$ hours.

Edexcel

The subject area covered is *Scientific Horizons (Science, Mathematics and Technology)*. A total of 50 marks are available for three sets of questions.

- Section A consists of about five **compulsory short-answer questions** worth between 1 and 5 marks each on key topics for this part of the specification. It is worth 17 marks in total.

- Section B is based on a passage of about 500 words and has three **compulsory short-answer comprehension questions** worth between 2 and 4 marks each plus 3 marks for overall quality of written communication, giving a total of 13 marks.

- Section C is a choice of one from three **essay questions on key topics**. It is worth 20 marks.

- Total time allowed is $1^1/4$ hours.

OCR

The subject area covered is *The Scientific Domain (Science, Mathematics and Technology)*. 100 marks are available over three sets of questions.

- The first question in Section A consists of a number of **compulsory short-answer comprehension questions** worth 20 marks in total, based on some figures, formulae or data. The second question is a compulsory piece of **extended writing** to explain basic scientific or mathematical principles and is worth 30 marks.

- Section B is a choice of one from three **two-part essay questions on key topics** for the unit, worth 50 marks. The first part requires you to define or describe a concept for 10 marks and the second to discuss aspects of it for 40 marks.

- Total time allowed is $1^1/4$ hours.

THE PROBLEM OF WASTE

(1) Waste is any substance that is no longer required. With increasing population, and especially with increasing prosperity, the amount of waste produced by a society increases.

(2) There are various categories of waste: it may be inert, biodegradable or hazardous. Inert substances, if put into landfill sites, will not break down. Glass, builder's rubble and plastic are inert. Biodegradable waste can be broken down by bacteria; it will usually be of organic origin such as food scraps, garden waste, or paper. Aerobic breakdown of organic matter produces carbon dioxide; anaerobic breakdown may produce methane. Hazardous wastes are those that pose a danger to humans. They will include spent nuclear fuel and other lower level nuclear waste, medical wastes which may be contaminated by pathogens, and chemical wastes which may themselves be toxic, or which may break down, or react with other chemicals, to form toxic products. These will include substances such as unused pesticides, acids and heavy metals, for example lead or cadmium. One particular hazardous waste is the carcasses of BSE-affected cattle. The infective prion protein that is thought to cause the disease is so persistent that it cannot be disposed of in landfill sites, and can only be burned and destroyed at exceptionally high temperatures.

(3) Some substances, such as plastics, which are otherwise inert, can produce harmful gases if they are burned inefficiently. Dioxins are released which are believed to cause infertility; their other health effects are not fully understood, but they are believed to be harmful. Biodegradable plastics have been developed, but are expensive.

(4) The UK produces an estimated 423 million tonnes of waste each year, of which 7% is municipal waste (MW) – which is produced in our homes and collected by the local council. The government does not control the waste from mining, quarrying and agriculture, but the disposal of other wastes is controlled by legislation, so that they can be disposed of only in ways and places that are regulated (Figure 1). Most municipal waste is disposed of in landfill sites (Figure 2).

(5) During their operation landfill sites are noisy, smelly and unsightly. They attract vermin such as rats, and are often invaded by seagulls. The constant arrival and departure of waste lorries causes increased risk of road accidents. The value of local housing falls. There has been a reduction in the number of landfill sites from 3400 in 1994 to 1500 in 1999, but the sites have become larger. As well as the local problems caused during working of the site, other problems arise. There is the risk that chemicals may be released into surface and underground water, and into soil; and that even after the site has been filled, covered with soil and landscaped, it may retain contaminants, or be unstable, and be unsuitable for some uses. Organic waste in landfills decomposes in anaerobic conditions to release methane gas. This is very flammable, so there is a risk of explosion if it collects in a confined area. It is also a powerful greenhouse gas, many times more effective than carbon dioxide. 27% of UK emissions of methane come from landfill sites. It is for this reason that European legislation requires the UK to reduce the use of landfill. It is possible to tap off the gas from landfill sites and use it either for local heating, or for power

generation; however, this is quite an expensive process so savings made are low. In order to discourage the use of landfill, costs have been increased and a landfill tax has been imposed. Unfortunately this has lead to an increase in illegal dumping (fly tipping).

(6) If the amount of material disposed of in landfill sites is to be reduced then obviously other methods of waste disposal need to be found. The methods currently used in the UK are incineration and recycling; each has benefits and disadvantages.

(7) Incineration is relatively inexpensive; it can be used to generate electricity; some of the ash produced can be used as aggregate; but it releases carbon dioxide, and can release harmful gases (e.g. dioxins) into the atmosphere if plastics such as PVC are burned.

(8) Recycling, although environmentally generally beneficial, may be more expensive than producing new materials. In the case of aluminium, recycling is economically viable because of the very high costs of obtaining the metal from its ore. However, in 1998, of the 5 billion aluminium cans used in the UK, 3.2 billion were sent to landfill sites. In the case of steel, transport and collection costs make recycling a much less economic alterative and the UK recycles very little steel. The UK has a poor record on recycling compared to other European countries; however, some local authorities within the UK have a much better record than others and recycling produces employment opportunities.

(9) Composting is another alternative to recycling for organic waste. It produces a valuable organic fertiliser, although the materials put into composters need to be carefully sorted to prevent a build-up of toxic chemicals such as heavy metals.

(10) No matter what other methods are used to dispose of waste a certain amount will always have to be put in landfill sites. This will be waste that is either non-biodegradable, or waste which cannot, or cannot safely, be burned. In addition, many hazardous materials need to be disposed of in special landfill sites where there is no risk of them escaping into the atmosphere, soil or water.

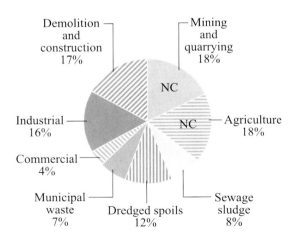

Figure 1 Estimated annual waste in the UK by sector (% of total mass). NC = Non-controlled

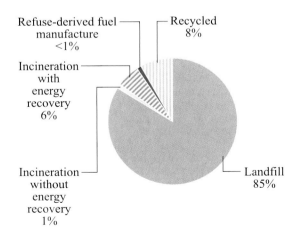

Figure 2 Treatment and disposal of municipal waste in the UK 1997/98

Question types 1, 4 and 13

Each of the questions carries 1 mark.

Read the passage entitled **THE PROBLEM OF WASTE** and answer the questions asked or implied by choosing the answer represented by the letter **A–D** which you think best.

1. What is the major hazard from medical waste (paragraph 2)?

    A   X-rays

    B   toxic chemicals

    C   disease organisms

    D   heavy metals

2. Which two categories of waste are the most likely to be inert (paragraph 2)?

    A   dredged spoils and sewage sludge

    B   municipal and agricultural

    C   commercial and industrial

    D   construction and quarrying

3. Which of the following explains why BSE carcasses could be hazardous in a landfill site (paragraphs 2 and 5)?

    1   Prion proteins could get into the water supply.

    2   Prion proteins could get into plants and be eaten by animals.

    3   Prion proteins are broken down only at very high temperatures.

    4   Scavengers might eat the carcasses and spread the disease.

    Answer
    A   **1** only
    B   **2** and **3** only
    C   **1** and **4** only
    D   all of them

4. Approximately how many million tonnes of waste not controlled by legislation are produced annually in the UK (paragraph 4 and Figure 1)?

    A   17

    B   76

    C   152

    D   271

5. What is the approximate ratio of landfill to recycled municipal waste (Figure 2)?

    A   8 : 1

    B   8.5 : 1

    C   10 : 1

    D   100 : 1

6. Which of the following best explains why it is less harmful for the global environment to burn methane than to release it (paragraph 5)?

   A   It destroys the ozone layer.

   B   It causes acid rain.

   C   It is a powerful greenhouse gas.

   D   Leaks can cause explosions.

7. Which statement explains why it may be harmful for pesticides to reach surface or underground water (paragraph 5)?

   A   They disrupt the food chain in rivers.

   B   They destroy water plant life.

   C   They promote excessive growth in water plants.

   D   They are pathogens.

8. Which greenhouse gas(es) is/are most likely to be emitted from incineration (paragraph 7)?

   1   dioxin

   2   radon

   3   methane

   4   carbon dioxide

   Answer
   A   **1** and **2** only
   B   **1, 2** and **3** only
   C   **2, 3** and **4** only
   D   **4** only

9. Which of the following types of waste disposal could help generation of power?

   1   recycling

   2   landfill

   3   incineration

   4   composting

   Answer
   A   **1** and **2** only
   B   **2** and **3** only
   C   **3** and **4** only
   D   all of them

10. Which of the following best explains why **changes in attitude** are required for recycling to become more popular in the UK?

   A   Everyone supports recycling but no-one will make the effort.

   B   Recycling is expensive.

   C   There are not enough recycling facilities.

   D   Some people are prepared to support recycling but others are not.

Question	Correct answer	Examiner's hints
1.	C	This is not a difficult question but you have to **be precise about both the wording of the question and the text** in paragraph 2. 'Medical' should lead you to either A or D (X-rays or disease organisms) and 'waste' to D. Many candidates opt wrongly for B (toxic chemicals), perhaps because it sounds the most hazardous? **Pathogens are organisms that cause disease**.
2.	D	'Inert' is **defined for you** in paragraph 2 – 'will not break down' – and described in the same paragraph – 'glass, builder's rubble and plastic'. The category that fits most closely is D (construction and quarrying).
3.	D	Here you need to consider what is said in paragraph 2 about BSE carcasses and prion proteins and in paragraph 5 about the dangers of landfill sites. Contaminants can **enter the water supply** (1), **go into soil** and therefore plants and be eaten by animals (2), **prion proteins can only be destroyed at very high temperatures** (3) and **landfill sites are often invaded** by scavengers, such as seagulls and rats (4). All are correct, so D is the answer.
4.	C	This is a **simple percentage calculation** but you have to draw the required data from both paragraph 4 and Figure 1. Paragraph 4 states that the total annual waste is estimated at 423 million tonnes and Figure 1 shows a total of 36% of waste not controlled by legislation (agriculture plus mining and quarrying). 36% of 423 = 152.28 = Option C.
5.	C	To answer this question you need to **understand what a ratio represents**. It is the relationship between two similar magnitudes – in this case the percentage of municipal waste disposed of by landfill (shown as 85% in Figure 2) compared with the percentage recycled (8%). To reduce the smaller quantity to 1 you have to divide by 8. You should then divide the other quantity by 8, and 85 divided by 8 = 10.625. The closest of the options is C (10 : 1).
6.	C	The question refers to harm to 'the global environment' and even if you are not entirely sure about greenhouse gases and other environmental threats (although you should be) **you can deduce the answer** from paragraph 5 ('methane … is also a powerful greenhouse gas, many times more effective than carbon dioxide'). Answers A (ozone layer) and B (acid rain) are not relevant. Answer D (explosions) is true, but these are a local and not a global threat. This leaves C (greenhouse gas) as the correct answer.
7.	A	In science comprehension **the precise meaning of words is extremely important**. 'Pesticides' are designed to eradicate 'pests' that are harmful to agriculture, usually insects. They have nothing to do with plants, so this rules out options B and C. Pesticides are chemical poisons and not disease bearing, which rules out D. So you can use a process of elimination to work out that the correct answer is A. Pesticides disrupt the food chain in rivers because fish eat insects.
8.	D	This question focuses on emissions from incineration, which are discussed in paragraph 7. Some basic knowledge about (greenhouse) gases helps, but **you can deduce the correct answer from the information in the passage**. Dioxins and radon are poisonous and can cause cancers, but they are not greenhouse gases. When it is burnt, methane is not a greenhouse gas either, and so that leaves carbon dioxide (paragraph 7). So the correct answer is 4 only.

9. **B** Here you have to **go back over the paragraphs** from 5 onwards to see what each says about power generation. It can include tapping off the gas and burning it from landfill (2), and incineration (3), as both involve heat. Composting (4) produces a little heat but not enough for genuine power generation, and recycling (1) consumes power rather than generating it. That gives you answer B (2 and 3 only).

10. **D** The key phrase is '**changes in attitude**', which is why it is in bold in the question. Attitudes involve **value judgements**, and you have to consider which of the options **relates best** to attitudes and is **the most valid**. All the statements contain expressions of opinion and are value judgements of sorts, but C and B are claims that are more **factual**. In terms of validity A ('**no-one will make the effort**') is **not a true statement**, and so by process of elimination D is the most appropriate answer.

Don't forget ...

You should use the same overall approach here as for the multiple-choice Arts Comprehension in Unit 1. (See 'Tackling Multiple Choice Questions' on page 14.)

Make sure you can **recognise the relationship between cause and effect**, and draw valid conclusions.

Typical topics in addition to environmental issues might be: evolution, genetics, energy resources, weather systems.

To answer these questions you need to be able to **precisely interpret** the scientific meaning of words and **use logical thinking**.

You can prepare for this subject by **reading articles about scientific matters** in a broadsheet newspaper or in magazines such as *New Scientist* or *Scientific American*, and by watching scientific documentaries on television, such as *Horizon*.

Questions are designed to test your **accurate observation** of patterns and trends in sequential data and **interpretation** of graphs showing rates of change.

The knowledge and understanding of the basic science you need will not go beyond what you **should have covered at GCSE**.

You should be confident in carrying out **simple calculations** and handling **very large or small numbers** using scientific notation (e.g. $0.001 = 10^{-3}$).

You must be clear that you understand the information and arguments in the passage and related data in charts and figures.

These questions will test your ability to **analyse and manipulate** the information and data.

SHORT-ANSWER QUESTIONS

Question type 12

1 **(a)** The population of the world is estimated to be 6×10^9.
Express the size of the world's population in millions. [1 mark]

NICK'S ANSWER

6 000 MILLION

 ¹/₁

(b) The dimensions of cells are often expressed in microns. A micron is 10^{-6} metre.
How many microns are there in a metre? [1 mark]

NICK'S ANSWER

1 000 000 MICRONS

 ¹/₁

Question type 1

2 Which of the following medical procedures does not create a potential ethical
problem for a doctor? [1 mark]

(a) Blood transfusions

(b) Heart transplants

(c) Kidney transplants

(d) Using antibiotics

NICK'S ANSWER

(d)

 ¹/₁

Question type 2

3 **(a)** Name a scientist who radically changed established ideas in a major aspect of
the physical sciences.
(b) State briefly the nature and importance of his or her discovery. [4 marks]

NICK'S ANSWER

(a) Sir Isaac Newton
(b) The theory of gravity

 ¹/₄

4 Percentages are often quoted in the media and advertisements to support an argument. Using two examples, show how percentages can be misleading. [6 marks]

NICK'S ANSWER

One way in which percentages can be misleading is that they might not state the total number. For example, a % might say that 70% might like or dislike something. 70% sounds a lot but not if only 50 people are asked. Statistically, that would be virtually meaningless.

3/6

How to score full marks

 1. (a) **You are allowed to use a calculator for questions of this type**, and this calculation was straightforward. **Alternative ways** of expressing the answer are either **six thousand million** or **6,000,000,000**.

(b) This is another fairly basic calculation. Nick could also have used these **alternative ways of expressing the answer:** one million or 10^6.

2. **Eliminate the options to reach the correct answer**. Blood transfusions (a) would not necessarily raise ethical problems, but they may be against a patient's religious beliefs. Transplants (b) and (c) do have the potential to raise ethical problems, especially if a part is to be transplanted from an animal to a human being, or because of the sensitivity of seeking permission from relatives of a dead person to use donor organs.

3. Nick either **didn't understand what this question required** or simply **didn't know enough basic science**. Sir Isaac Newton certainly was an eminent physical scientist associated with the law of Universal Gravity (which he is said to have developed after watching apples fall from a tree). Newton developed a gravity model, which can be expressed in a formula. **Nick needed to be clear about this** to get a further mark and to **use an example** of the use of the gravity model for full marks. He might have used orbits of planets and stars (where the model was used in the Apollo mission in 1970 after the spacecraft's four main systems failed) or the way in which social scientists have borrowed Newton's formula to predict the movement of people between two centres (perhaps between two urban areas).

4. Nick did the first half of the answer very well, gaining 1 mark for the example and a further 2 marks for the detailed explanation. **A second example and explanation would have brought full marks**. He might have explained the importance of a percentage increase depending on the initial number or the extent to which percentages might be out of date.

Don't forget ...

Multiple-choice questions have **only one** answer.

Unless you have absolutely no idea, try to **write something more extensive** for questions like 3(b), or to **make two points where two are required**.

DATA QUESTIONS

Look carefully at the table below and answer the questions which follow.

Atmospheric pollutants

Estimated UK emission of primary pollutants for 1989 measured in units of 10^6 tonnes

Source	Black smoke	Sulphur dioxide	Nitrogen oxides	Carbon monoxide	Volatile organic compounds (excluding methane)
Domestic	191	138	68	339	50
Industrial	81	683	353	331	1435*
Power stations	25	2640	769	47	12
Refineries	2	109	35	1	107
Petrol road vehicles	15	22	848	6182	727
Diesel road vehicles	182	38	580	160	160
Railways	–	3	32	12	8
Gas leakage (during distribution)	–	–	–	–	34
Other	4	88	157	31	18
Total emissions	**500**	**3721**	**2842**	**7103**	**2551**

*Includes evaporation of motor spirit during storage and distribution

Question type 12

1. According to the table what percentage of total emissions was produced by carbon monoxide? [2 marks]

KERRY'S ANSWER

The emission level resulting from carbon monoxide is 7103 units. The total emission level from all other sources is 9614 units. As a percentage this is 42%

Question types 15, 16

2. What conclusions can you draw from the comparative figures for petrol and diesel as pollutants? [2 marks]

KERRY'S ANSWER

Petrol is worse for carbon monoxide but diesel is worse for black smoke emissions. The figures are for 1989 — the move towards lead-free petrol to cut emissions is understandable.

3. There is a general belief that the British government have taken action to tackle the problems of atmospheric pollutants. How far is this belief backed up by the data in the table and by developments since 1989?   [8 marks]

KERRY'S ANSWER

Obviously some monitoring of the situation regarding pollutants has taken place otherwise the table wouldn't exist though it is clear from the table that some sources contribute little. All the main political parties support green policies. Lead-free petrol has been brought in and now almost everyone uses it.

On the other hand large amounts of emissions still occur today and it would be useful to see more up-to-date figures. Pollution of the environment is still a big

5/8

How to score full marks

1. Kerry had no problems with question 1, gaining a mark each for **showing her method** and giving the correct answer. (42.48% was the actual answer but marks would be given for either 42% or 43%.)

2. Kerry wrote two brief **factual sentences** for 2 marks.

3. Kerry gained a mark in a mark band which indicated that she made a 'competent average response showing some understanding of the limitations of statistical knowledge with satisfactory expression'. She needed a **slightly longer** answer to reach full marks. She might have been **more explicit** about government policies, perhaps mentioning stricter rules on exhaust limits for MOTs or clean air legislation.

4. Kerry did state that the information in the statistical tables was **dated**. She might have said that statistical tables offer only a **snapshot** at certain times and that some of the worst emissions are **petrol-based carbon monoxide** from vehicles and industrial pollutants such as **sulphur dioxide from power stations**. This might have led her to **question the commitment of governments** or the **effectiveness of their policies**.

Don't forget ...

Always **show your working** if calculations are required.

Look at the marks available to decide how many points you need to make. You may need to make two brief points if 2 marks are available.

Learn as much as you can about the **origins, compilation, use and limitations of statistical tables**. Though they are informative you need to **think about them critically** and **remember that they rarely contain any explanation of the figures**.

Question types 2, 3, 9, 10, 11

Answer the question below by writing a short paragraph in continuous prose.

'The benefits of the mobile phone far outweigh its drawbacks.'

How far do you agree with this assertion?   [12 marks]

Wayne followed the instructions of the question and wrote a short paragraph of continuous prose. There were some spelling mistakes but the meaning is reasonably clear. Wayne has made several points both for and against, although these points are not always well structured. In some cases, he has over-personalised some of his material when it might have been helpful to have remained more detached.

WAYNE'S ANSWER

Few teenagers are seen without a mobile phone these days because it makes them seem cool. It's amazing how much technology has moved ahead in only a few years. My mum and dad often remark that things are now very different. When they were you nobody had a mobile phone. Now everybody does and if theyre not on the phone they are sending text messages. You can easily carry them round and contact your friends quickly if youre going to be late. People use them for all sorts of things. One big problem is crime cos lots of people have had theirs stolen. They can be quiet a lot of money. My parents got one for my sister to keep her safe. Some people even say that they damage your health but I wouldn't be without mine nor would lots of teenagers.

6/12

How to score full marks

Wayne's paragraph contained both **benefits** and **drawbacks** as the question required, but he **didn't have enough of either.**

- Among the **benefits,** Wayne might have been **more specific** about the convenience of the mobile phone and the ways in which in can be used. He could also have mentioned **WAP** (Wireless Application Protocol) phones, which give access to internet, TV, etc., a **feeling of independence** and the **privacy** associated with text messages.

- **Drawbacks** might have included a more **specific reference to health** (potential brain damage); **radiation** sometimes linked with transmission masts; dangers associated with **using a phone while driving**; **peer group pressure** to buy expensive phones or to keep up with changing fashions and the **corruption of language** which might result from text messaging.

Wayne needed to make sure that his knowledge was translated into **clearer and crisper arguments.** Not all of the points could be included in a short paragraph but he needed to **balance benefits and drawbacks.**

It is important to **write accurately** and to **avoid spelling mistakes** and **abbreviations** like 'cos'.

Wayne did arrive at a **conclusion** but his **over-personalised style** limited its effectiveness.

Don't forget ...

Do what the question says – in this case that meant writing a short paragraph. You cannot include everything in a short answer and the examiner will **not be able to give you more marks than those printed on the question paper.**

Use the question as an aid. Highlight the **key words** and, if you find it helpful, **sketch a brief plan**.

Look out for words like **'assertion'.** It reflects a view or opinion, not a fact. Always be ready to **challenge assertions**. You **do not have to agree** if you can produce **evidence** and **logical arguments** to the contrary.

Try to **resist personalising material.** Too many **anecdotal/personal** examples might suggest a **limited range and depth of knowledge**.

Try to reach a **clear conclusion** when you are asked to say how far you agree with a statement. Your conclusion **need not be absolutely definite**, especially if the points for and against are **finely balanced.**

ESSAY QUESTIONS

Question types 3, 9, 10, 11

Answer the following question:

'Unethical forms of medical research should be prohibited even if they provide solutions to social and medical problems.'

To what extent do you agree with this claim? [17 marks]

There will be an additional 3 marks for the quality of written communication.

> **This is a useful opening. It indicates that medical research can be newsworthy, although the paragraph doesn't refer to the ethics concerned.**

> **Helen is now getting closer to possible ethical dilemmas but she is tending to describe a form of research that might be unethical when she needs to be evaluating it.**

> **Helen hasn't quite clinched the point. The transplantation of animal parts into humans is often considered unethical but Helen needs to say why. Then she should compare this with the value we place on saving a human life.**

> **Helen seeks to provide an example of unethical research. The examples needed to be a little more explicit and the dilemmas needed more emphasis.**

> **A good attempt at a conclusion. Helen might have tried to answer the two questions she poses but, in circumstances of life and death, the end might justify the means.**

HELEN'S ANSWER

Medical research is often reported on in the newspapers and we are told that technology is advancing all the time. Often these are the 'big news' stories such as a transplant though most people are interested more in the human angle than the technical details of any research.

People often have strong views about certain kinds of research and this is often the case if it involves cloning. Much has been written about Dolly the sheep and cloning. This doesn't seem to be as serious as some stories about experiments with stem cells. This could lead to designer babies and the feeling that doctors might be playing God.

This is where research can become unethical. We are taught to trust scientists because they are qualified people who do serious research in laboratories. Medical research should be for the good of the people and there have been many advances such as transplants. This shows how research can save the lives of people but there has been talk of transplanting animal parts into humans. That would be unethical.

It can be very difficult to watch over everything that doctors are doing and the Nazis did some terrible experiments with people in World War 2. There was a place called Porton Down in England where soldiers volunteered to help with medical research which was dangerous. The soldiers weren't told this and some died. This was unethical. It was the sort of work done in secret that you would want to stop.

There have been big advances in medicine and nobody would want to stop this. If something is unethical it should be stopped but who decides what is ethical and who decides if it should be stopped? People who are very ill and their families are likely to value life. They may not think that something that saves their life is unethical. Staying alive may justify the method.

9+2/20

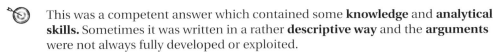

How to score full marks

- This was a competent answer which contained some **knowledge** and **analytical skills.** Sometimes it was written in a rather **descriptive way** and the **arguments** were not always fully developed or exploited.

- Helen opened by making the point about **media interest** in medical research and the importance of the human angle. She might have **changed the emphasis** of her opening paragraph so that the 'human angle' included a direct reference to what might be considered as **ethical** or **unethical** research.

- **The potential of the second paragraph was not fully realised.** Both 'cloning' and the notion of 'doctors playing God' are important. Helen included both but did not really show how either might be deemed unethical, perhaps in terms of **personal values** or **religious beliefs.**

- This weakness was repeated in the third paragraph. Helen recognised the **fundamental aim of medical research** and transplants raise a range of **ethical issues**. It was some of these that she needed to focus on, saying **why** there are concerns about the possibility of using organs from animals for transplantation into humans.

- Helen's fourth paragraph was of more limited relevance, partly because the **references** to Nazi experiments and Porton Down were **vague** and partly because she didn't **show clearly why** the work was unethical.

- Helen's conclusion did seek to show how **the preservation of human life** might make ethical dilemmas seem less significant but, on the whole, her essay **didn't contain enough arguments and counter arguments.** She had some relevant knowledge but needed to use this in a more **analytical** way and one which focused more directly on the **central issue** – the question of **whether or not certain forms of medical research should be prohibited even if they provide solutions to social and medical problems**.

- Helen needed to **use some of the examples she mentioned in this context.** Some aspects of research can be very **emotive** – for example research that involves human embryos. Equally, if it is properly conducted and adequately supervised, **stem cell research** can offer many positive outcomes to people who might suffer crippling and life-threatening diseases. Doctors and scientists must have some **professional freedom** to undertake research but this may be **difficult to monitor on an international basis.** The potential for **huge financial rewards** may encourage **unethical methods with unwanted/unanticipated outcomes**.

Don't forget ...

Define your terms – say what you think words like **unethical** mean.

Make sure your knowledge is always addressed directly at the question asked.

Don't describe when you should be seeking to analyse/evaluate. Questions often ask **how far you agree** with a viewpoint expressed.

Don't assume that there is a 'right' answer that you must find. Ethical dilemmas are very complex and there is rarely a way of proving that a conclusion is 'right' or 'wrong'. What really count are **the range and quality of arguments** and your ability to use them logically to **reach a conclusion that follows from the arguments.**

Try to set out your arguments and counter-arguments. There are usually 'two sides' to each question. Try to balance the two sets of arguments and use them to reach a conclusion.

Question types 1, 12, 13

Each of the questions carries 1 mark.

Answer the questions asked or implied by choosing the answer represented by the letter **A–D** which you think best.

A small catering firm makes the following charges for providing a buffet.

    For up to 50 people: £50 plus £3 per person

    For 51 to 100 people: £200 plus £2 per person in excess of 50

These charges can be written as formulae as follows:

$$C = 50 + 3N \qquad \text{for } N \leq 50$$
$$C = 200 + 2(N - 50) \qquad \text{for } 50 < N \leq 100$$

where N is the number of people catered for and the cost is £C.

1.   The cost of a buffet for 80 people is

    A   £140

    B   £260

    C   £290

    D   £360

2.   A correct rearrangement of the second formula is

    A $N = \dfrac{C - 200}{2} + 50$

    B $N = \dfrac{C - 2}{200} + 50$

    C $N = \dfrac{C - 200 - 2}{50}$

    D $N = \dfrac{C}{2} - 200 + 50$

3.   A car's value depreciated at a rate of 12% per year. When new it cost £9750. Its value to the nearest £50 after 3 years was

    A   £6259

    B   £6650

    C   £6900

    D   £13 700

4. It is necessary to convert a length in feet to its approximate equivalent in millimetres. Taking $2^1/2$ centimetres to be 1 inch, you should multiply by which of the following?

A $\dfrac{1000}{3}$

B   300

C $\dfrac{100}{3}$

D $\dfrac{1}{300}$

5. The diagram shows a circle with a diameter CB of length 5 cm and a tangent AT of length 6 cm.

Which of the following is the length of AB?

A   3.5 cm

B   4 cm

C   4.5 cm

D   5 cm

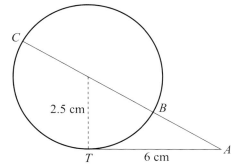

6. The ages in years of 10 horses in a stable were

      3, 3, 4, 5, 7, 7, 7, 8, 8, 8

Which one of the following is true?

A   mean = median

B   mean > median > range

C   median > range > mean

D   median > mean > range

7. The table shows data about the students in a class.

	Male	Female
Wears glasses	5	7
Doesn't wear glasses	11	6

What is the probability that a male student picked at random wears glasses?

A $\dfrac{5}{29}$

B $\dfrac{5}{16}$

C $\dfrac{5}{12}$

D $\dfrac{5}{11}$

8. A driver travels along a road with velocity as shown by the velocity–time graph.

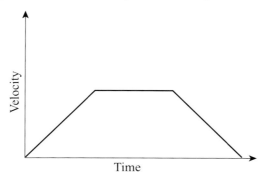

The most appropriate sketch of the distance–time graph for this journey is

A

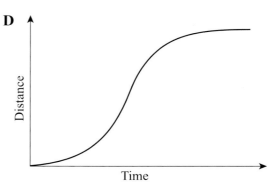

B

C

D

9. A network of railway lines is made up as shown with the length of each section as indicated.

What is the shortest route from *S* to *Z*?

  A 8

  B 9

  C 10

  D 11

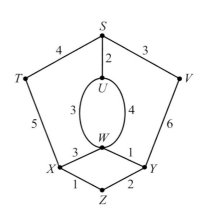

10. A football team which plays 38 games in a season gets 3 points for winning, 1 point for drawing and 0 points for losing. The manager sets the team a target of getting at least 70 points and not losing more than 10 games in the season. The number of games won is x and the number of games drawn is y. Which one of the following pairs of inequalities represents this target?

A $3x + y \le 70$ $x + y \le 28$

B $3x + y \ge 70$ $x + y \ge 28$

C $3x + y > 70$ $x + y > 28$

D $3x + y \ge 70$ $x + y < 28$

11. A game board consists of 16 identical squares as shown.

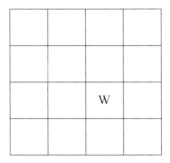

A player starts at square W, shown in the diagram, and makes moves. The only moves allowed are 1 square diagonally in any direction. Which of the following shows, as shaded, all the possible positions which could be occupied after **exactly two** moves?

A

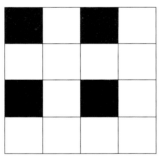

B

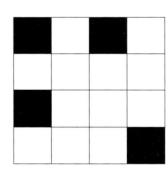

C

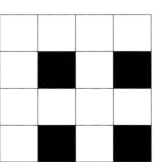

D

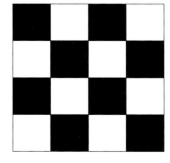

12. Which one of the following is a sketch graph of $y = x^2 - 5x - 6$?

A
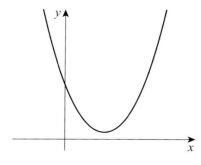

C
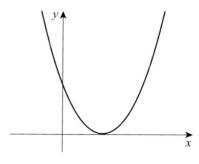

B
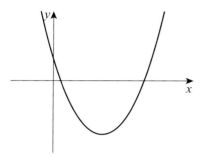

D
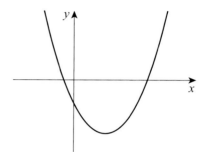

13. At a college, students are given a points score calculated from their GCSE grades.

Someone with 4 A grades and 4 B grades gains a score of 36 points.

Someone with 2 A grades and 4 B grades gains a score of 26 points.

Someone with 3 A grades and 3 B grades would have a score of:

  A 21 points

  B 27 points

  C 30 points

  D 31 points

14. The ages of two friends are in the ratio 3 : 4. In 8 years time their ages will be in the ratio 5 : 6. How old are they now?

  A 3, 4

  B 6, 8

  C 9, 12

  D 12, 16

15. Golzow is west of Kanin. Kanin is north of Ragewitz. Which range of bearings must include the bearing of Golzov from Ragewitz?

  A 000° to 090°

  B 090° to 180°

  C 180° to 270°

  D 270° to 360°

Question	Correct answer	Examiner's hints

Calculations

1.   **B**   This is a matter of **identifying and applying the appropriate formula**. There are 80 people, so the second method should be chosen, and the calculation done **in the correct order**:

$$C = 200 + 2(N - 50) \quad \text{brackets first}$$
$$= 200 + 2 \times 30 \quad \text{then multiplication}$$
$$= 200 + 60 = 260$$

Re-arrangement of formulae

2.   **A**   As in question 1, the solution relies on identifying the correct order – in this case **finding the inverse ('opposite') of each step**, in reverse order to that shown in question 1.

N is required, so remove the other terms by rearranging the equation:

$$C = 200 + 2(N - 50)$$
$$C - 200 = 2(N - 50)$$
$$\frac{C - 200}{2} = N - 50$$
$$\frac{C - 200}{2} + 50 = N$$

Percentages

3.   **B**   A common error here is to assume that the actual decrease in value each year is the same (constant). One correct method is to find 12%, subtract this from the value that year to find a new value, and repeat this a further two times. **An alternative, and much quicker**, way is to realise that if the car loses 12% of its value each year, then it retains 88%. Finding 88% of a quantity can be done by multiplying by 0.88, so finding the value after 3 years is done by

$$0.88 \times 0.88 \times (0.88 \times \pounds 9750), \text{ or just } 0.88^3 \times \pounds 9750.$$

Response B (£6650) is closest to this value.

Conversions

4.   **B**   This question relies on **combining two conversion factors, by multiplying fractions**. It may be easiest to consider the changes in stages, from feet to inches ($\times 12$), inches to centimetres ($\times 2^{1}/_{2}$, i.e. $\times \, ^{5}/_{2}$), and centimetres to millimetres ($\times 10$). The overall multiplying factor is

$$12 \times {}^{5}/_{2} \times 10 = 300.$$

Alternatively 1 inch is 25 mm, so 12 inches is 300 mm.

Geometry/trigonometry

5.   **B**   This relies on realising that, as the diameter is 5 cm, the dashed line must be a radius, and therefore that the angle at T (between a radius and a tangent) must be 90°. The hypotenuse of the triangle can be found **using Pythagoras' theorem**, and then subtracting the length of the radius to find AB. (Note the diagram is not drawn to scale.)

Statistics

6.   **D**   This question should be straightforward if you remember the rules for finding the terms correctly.

Mean = **sum of all the ages**, divided by the number of horses (i.e. ages)
$$= 60 \div 10 = 6$$

Median = **Middle value** when ages are in order (as they are here)

= age between 5th and 6th
(so there will be five ages to the left, and five to the right)

= between 7 and 7, i.e. 7

Range = **largest age minus smallest age**

= 8 − 3 = 5

Probability

7. **B** The table gives information about all the students in a class (29 students). However, the question **refers only to *male* students**, of whom there are 16. Of these 16 males, 5 wear glasses. Hence the probability is

$$\frac{\text{no. of males wearing glasses}}{\text{total no. of males}} = \frac{5}{16}$$

Graphs (speed/time/distance)

8. **D** This is a matter of interpreting the initial velocity–time graph. The central section shows that the **velocity is constant**, so for this part of the journey the distance travelled will increase at a constant rate. For the first part of the journey the **velocity is increasing**, so in any one second, for example, the car will be travelling faster than it was in the previous second, and so travel a greater distance. The distance–time graph must therefore be rising faster and faster at this stage, curving upwards. In the final section the car travels at a **slower and slower rate**, and so the distance will increase less and less.

Networks

9. **A** This relies on tracing through all the possible paths, and taking account of the numbers on each stretch of path, and not being influenced by the actual length of the lines in the drawing. **It helps to be systematic.**

The shortest distance from *S* to *W* is 5.

So from *S* to *Y* is either 5 + 1 (via *W*) or 3 + 6 (via *V*), i.e. 6.

From *S* to *X* is either 4 + 5 (via *T*) or 5 + 3 (via *W*) i.e. 8.

The shortest path from *S* to *Z* via *X* is 8 + 1 = 9

and from *S* to *Z* via *Y* is 6 + 2 = 8, the required response.

Inequalities

10. **B** The two conditions arise from the **number of points and the number of games**.

Winning *x* games gets $x \times 3 = 3x$ points, drawing *y* games gets $y \times 1 = y$ points.

The manager therefore requires

$3x + y \geq 70$ ('at least' 70 implies that equalling 70 will be acceptable)

Winning *x* and drawing *y* means that the remainder $38 - x - y$ are lost.

Therefore we require $38 - x - \leq 10$ ('not more' means 10 is acceptable)

Rearranging this inequality gives $38 \leq 10 + x + y$ and hence $28 \leq x + y$.

Thus $x + y \geq 28$ = Option B.

Logic

11. **A** This question is probably best answered by first considering which squares might be occupied after **exactly one** move. This gives the possible, shaded, positions as shown in the diagram. By now considering the possibilities from each of the shaded squares in turn, you can see that the possibilities after two moves are those shown in response A. It is vital that you interpret the wording of the question precisely – the possible positions **after exactly two** moves.

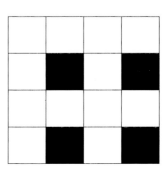

Graphs (formulae)

12. D You can tackle this question in various ways. The 'expected' method would probably be to **factorise the expression** $x^2 - 5x - 6 = (x - 6)(x + 1)$. The curve will cross the x axis when $x = 6$ and when $x = -1$. However, when $x = 0$, $y = 0 - 0 - 6 = -6$ and there is only one diagram where the curve crosses the y axis at a negative value.

Algorithms/simultaneous equations

13. B There are two methods for solving this question. A standard method would be to **form two simultaneous equations**.

$$4a + 4b = 36, \text{ and}$$

$$2a + 4b = 26$$

subtracting gives $2a = 10$, so $a = 5$

and with a little further work using either equation $b = 4$. Hence the result.

However, in this particular example four As and four Bs score 36 points, so one A and one B must together therefore score 9 points, a quarter of 36, then three As and three Bs must score three-quarters of 36, namely 27.

Ratios

14. D In practice this might best be done by taking each possible answer, adding 8 and then seeing if the resulting ages are in the ratio 5 : 6.

For students who prefer an **analytical approach**, let the ages be $3x$ and $4x$.

Then $\dfrac{3x + 8}{4x + 8} = \dfrac{5}{6}$, so 'cross-multiplying' gives $18x + 48 = 20x + 40$.

This leads to $2x = 8$, hence $x = 4$, and so the ages are $3 \times 4 = 12$ and $4 \times 4 = 16$.

Bearings

15. D It is crucial that you **draw a correct diagram** giving the relative positions:

Golzow   Kanin

Ragewitz

You must then take the bearing **from** Ragewitz, so imagine standing there facing north, and then see what angle (clockwise) you would need to turn through in order to face Golzow.

Don't forget ...

Most mathematical reasoning questions are based on **GCSE Mathematics (Higher) knowledge and understanding**.

If there is a question you are not sure about, leave it and **move on to later questions. Make sure you have time to go back** to questions you have left out. Guess the answers if necessary!

The 15 questions given here are **typical of the range** of mathematical topics/applications tested. For more practice look at some past papers.

It is well worth particularly **revising the mathematical topics/applications you find hardest** or are not sure about.

HYDROGEN POWER

(1)   In most countries of the world, energy is obtained by combustion of fossil fuels (Figure 1a). However, within twenty years, Iceland aims to be the first country in the world to cut its links with fossil fuels and create a 'hydrogen economy', based on its most abundant resource – water. Energy analysts say it is a strategy that could turn this country of 270 000 people into one of the world's 'energy sheikhs' by the middle of the 21st century and, if adopted worldwide, would banish global warming.

(2)   Iceland's electricity comes largely from hydroelectric power, and it heats its buildings by tapping geothermal energy from hot volcanic rocks. Now it wants to wean its transport system away from oil. The new power source will be hydrogen, made by splitting water molecules using the island's abundant hydroelectric power. The hydrogen will be liquefied and fed to fuel cells that will power electrically driven buses, trucks, cars and even the fishing fleet. Within a few years, Icelandic hydrogen could be on sale at filling stations around the world.

(3)   In a modern fuel cell, a platinum electrode strips electrons from the hydrogen. The resulting hydrogen ions pass through an electrolyte to the opposite electrode. The electrons pass through an external circuit and then at the other electrode combine with the hydrogen ions and oxygen to produce water and electricity (Figure 1b). Vehicles running on fuel cells are quiet, more efficient and produce virtually none of the pollutants associated with petrol engines, such as nitrogen oxides and the greenhouse gas, carbon dioxide. Only water vapour comes out of the exhaust pipe, and as the fuel cell converts chemical energy directly into electrical energy, less waste heat is generated. The chief problems holding back this technology are cost, the difficulty of storing liquid hydrogen safely and packing enough on board to give the vehicle adequate range and power. A prototype new electric car travelled 400 kilometres without refuelling. Due to the difficulty of storing hydrogen, it carried methanol as its fuel, and used it to generate hydrogen in an on-board 'reformer' (Figure 1c). This hybrid technology splits methanol to produce hydrogen and carbon dioxide and is a halfway house to true hydrogen power.

(4)   Iceland sees itself as the ideal testing ground for a hydrogen economy. A small but wealthy island, with a vehicle fleet physically cut off from other countries, it is better placed than most to convert to hydrogen. It is also well placed to manufacture the fuel in an environmentally friendly way and to export it. The energy needed to split water molecules can come from any convenient source – although using coal or oil would largely defeat the object because it would maintain dependence on fossil fuels. Using renewable energy breaks the link, and Iceland is ideally placed to do this. A wet, mountainous country with plenty of fast-flowing rivers, it currently uses only a tenth of its hydroelectric potential.

(5) The big attraction of hydrogen is that it will help solve urban air quality problems. Whether it helps with climate change depends on how the hydrogen is made. If it is made using renewable energy then there are real attractions. The US government believes that if 10% of automobiles used hydrogen fuel cells instead of petrol engines, air pollutants would be cut by 1 million tons per year, 60 million tons of carbon dioxide would be eliminated and oil imports would be cut by 800 000 barrels per day (about 13% of total oil imports). Certainly there is huge potential for using hydrogen as a way of carrying power from remote sources of renewable energy, such as Arctic rivers, to where the demand is greatest. The day when we in Britain fill up with Icelandic hydrogen rather than Gulf oil may be nearer than we think.

Based on an article in *New Scientist* 1999

Figure 1 Chemical equations related to energy production

(a) **Exothermic combustion of fuels**

(Hydrogen) $\qquad$ $H_2 + \frac{1}{2}O_2 \rightarrow H_2O$ $\qquad$ $\Delta H = -286$ kJ mol^{-1}

(Methane) $\qquad$ $CH_4 + 2O_2 \rightarrow CO_2 + 2H_2O$ $\qquad$ $\Delta H = -890$ kJ mol^{-1}

(Methanol) $\qquad$ $CH_3OH + 1\frac{1}{2}O_2 \rightarrow CO_2 + H_2O$ $\qquad$ $\Delta H = -715$ kJ mol^{-1}

(Petrol) $\qquad$ $C_8H_{18} + 12\frac{1}{2}O_2 \rightarrow 8CO_2 + 9H_2O$ $\qquad$ $\Delta H = -5512$ kJ mol^{-1}

(b) **Fuel cell equations**

At anode (+ve electrode) $\qquad$ $2H_2 \rightarrow 4H^+ + 4e^-$

At cathode (−ve electrode) $\qquad$ $O_2 + 4H^+ + 4e^- \rightarrow 2H_2O$

Overall $\qquad$ $2H_2 + O_2 \rightarrow 2H_2O$

(c) **Reforming of methanol or methane into hydrogen using steam**

(Methanol) $\qquad$ $CH_3OH + H_2O \rightarrow CO_2 + 3H_2$

(Methane) $\qquad$ $CH_4 + 2H_2O \rightarrow CO_2 + 4H_2$

Question types 1, 4

Each of the questions carries 1 mark.

Read the passage and figures entitled **HYDROGEN POWER** and answer the questions asked or implied by choosing the answer represented by the letter **A–D** which you think best.

1. Which one of the following is the reason why using hydrogen might banish global warming (paragraph 1 and Figure 1a)?
   A   reduces damage to the ozone layer
   B   reduction in the production of CO_2
   C   water vapour would reduce greenhouse effect
   D   removal of hydrogen reduces greenhouse effect

2. Which one of the following would release the most energy (Figure 1a)?
   A   1 mole of petrol
   B   2 moles of methane
   C   10 moles of methanol
   D   20 moles of hydrogen

3. Which one of the following is the most efficient hydrocarbon fuel to supply to the reformer (Figure 1c)?
   A   hydrogen
   B   methane
   C   water
   D   alcohol

4. Why is Iceland keen to become the first 'hydrogen economy' (paragraph 4)?
   1   plentiful supply of water
   2   unused renewable energy
   3   no significant oil reserves
   4   large population
   A   **1** and **3** only
   B   **2** and **4** only
   C   **3** and **4** only
   D   **1**, **2** and **3** only

5. The environmental benefit derived from using the hybrid technology (paragraphs 3 and 4) is that it does **not** produce
   A   nitrogen oxides
   B   water vapour
   C   carbon dioxide
   D   global cooling

6. How many tons of air pollutants does the US government believe are put into the atmosphere annually by car petrol engines (paragraph 5)?

   A   0.1 million
   B   1 million
   C   10 million
   D   100 million

7. Which of the following is/are a probable consequence of global warming?

   1   climatic instability
   2   increase in flooding
   3   increase in insect pests
   4   increased skin cancer
   A   1 and 3 only
   B   2 and 4 only
   C   1 and 4 only
   D   1, 2 and 3 only

8. Which of the following statements about hydrogen is/are **always** true?

   1   a colourless gas
   2   less dense than air
   3   explodes when mixed with oxygen
   A   1 and 2 only
   B   1 and 3 only
   C   2 and 3 only
   D   none of them

9. Which of the following statements about the use of hydrogen as a fuel is an opinion rather than a scientific fact?

   1   The combustion of hydrogen does not contribute to global warming.
   2   Burning hydrogen in air produces fewer combustion products than burning methane in air.
   A   1 only
   B   2 only
   C   both of them
   D   neither of them

10. In the following question you are given an assertion followed by a reason. Consider both statements and decide whether each on its own is a true statement. Then, if both are true, consider whether the reason is a valid explanation of the assertion.

    Answer
    A   if the assertion is true, but the reason is false.
    B   if the assertion is false, but the reason is true.
    C   if both statements are true and the reason is a correct explanation of the assertion
    D   if both statements are true, but the reason is not a correct explanation of the assertion

Assertion		Reason
Vehicles powered by fuel cells are more efficient than those using internal combustion engines	*because*	in a fuel cell electricity is produced directly from chemical energy and less waste heat is generated.

Answers can be found on pages 87–88.

SHORT-ANSWER AND ESSAY QUESTIONS

Question type 2

1. Comment on the different ways in which the media have reported a scientific story.

[5 marks]

Question types 2, 12

2. Prime numbers can not be divided by any number other than 1. Find five examples, using different prime numbers greater than 3, to show the sum of two prime numbers gives an even number.

[5 marks]

Question types 6, 7, 10, 11

3. A small country came under the rule of a dictator. The dictator ruled from a strong fortress. The fortress was situated in the middle of the country, surrounded by farms and villages. Many roads radiated out from the fortress like the spokes of a wheel. A general raised an army to free the country. He knew that if all his army attacked at once the fortress could be captured. The general knew that the dictator had planted mines along each road and that a large force could detonate the mines though small groups could pass over them safely. The general defeated the dictator.

   (i) How did the general defeat the dictator? [6 marks]

   (i) What other factors would it have been useful for you to know to answer **(i)** more effectively? [4 marks]

 (iii) How might this problem be applied to real life? [2 marks]

Question types 3, 7, 8, 11

4. Though we have come to know a lot about what makes for health and fitness, we nevertheless lead unhealthy lives. How far would you agree that we should attach more importance to keeping fit?

You might consider the following in your answer:
- the costs of ill health
- the place of physical education in the school curriculum
- the relationship between fitness and health
- the freedom of the individual to be unfit.

[30 marks]

Question types 3, 7, 8, 9, 10, 11

5. **(a)** The average income of a group was £15 000, £20 000 and £22 500. Show how it is possible that all these figures can be correct. Explain any terms you use. [10 marks]

   (b) Disraeli said: 'There are lies, damned lies and statistics.' Outline ways in which statistics are useful and powerful but can also mislead. [40 marks]

Answers can be found on pages 88–91.

3 Society, Politics and the Economy

UNIT 3 EXAMINATIONS

AQA (Specification A)

The subject area covered is *Society, Politics and the Economy*. 50 marks are available for five questions set on **five sources linked to a common theme** (e.g. drugs, race relations, the monarchy).

● All questions are compulsory.
● Time allowed is $1^1/4$ hours.

AQA (Specification B)

The theme of this paper is *Space*. 60 marks are available for two questions, which are set on **data-based topics related to the theme of the paper**.

● Both questions are compulsory.
● Time allowed is $1^1/4$ hours.

Edexcel

The subject area specified is *Social Perspectives*.

● Section A contains **short-answer questions,** **mostly based on data sets**, with 17 marks available.
● Section B is based on **comprehension questions linked to a passage** and 13 marks are available.
● All questions in these sections are compulsory.
● In section C an **extended writing question**, for 20 marks, involves a choice of **one from three**.
● Time allowed is $1^1/2$ hours.

OCR

The subject is *The Social Domain (Society, Politics and the Economy)*.

● Section A contains **short questions based on two brief passages**. There are 50 marks and all questions are compulsory.
● In section B, students are asked to choose **one essay from three**. Each essay carries 50 marks.
● Time allowed is $1^1/4$ hours.

EXAM QUESTIONS AND ANSWERS

SHORT-ANSWER DATA SET QUESTIONS

● **Multiple choice** – very few in number and used only by **Edexcel**.
● **Calculations and interpretation** – used by **Edexcel and AQA**.
● **Comprehension** – used by **OCR and AQA (Specification A)**.

Answer each of the following questions based on the data relating to the changing composition of households between 1961 and 1991. Calculators may be used.

Households : by type of household and family

Great Britain	1961(%)	1971(%)	1981(%)	1991(%)
One person	11	18	22	27
Two or more unrelated adults	5	4	5	3
One-family households				
Couple with:				
No children	26	27	26	28
1–2 dependent children	30	26	25	20
3 or more dependent children	8	9	6	5
Non-dependent children only	10	8	8	8
Lone parent	6	7	9	10
Multi-family households	3	1	1	1
All households (= 100%) (millions)	**16.3**	**18.6**	**20.2**	**22.4**

Source: adapted from *Social Trends 1999*, page 42 Crown Copyright

Question types 12 and 14

(a) Calculate by how many **millions**

   (i) the total number of households rose between 1961 and 1991. [1 mark]

   (ii) the number of one-family households with 1–2 dependent children changed between 1971 and 1981. [1 mark]

(b) Calculate the **percentage** increase in the number of households

   (i) between 1961 and 1971. [1 mark]

   (ii) between 1981 and 1991. [1 mark]

(c) What conclusion can be drawn from your calculations? [2 marks]

ALAN'S ANSWERS

(a) (i) 22.4 − 16.3 = an increase of 6.1 million

   (ii) (25% x 20.2 = 5.05 million) − (26% x 18.6 = 4.83 million).
   Change is 0.22 million.

(b) (i) 18.6 − 16.3 = 2.3 divided by 16.3 = 14.11%

   (ii) 22.4 − 20.2 = 2.2 divided by 20.2 = 10.89%

(c) Things went up

How to score full marks

 (a) **(i)** Alan scored 1 mark for **subtracting** 16.3 million from 22.4 million.

   (ii) He then knew he had to **find the difference** between the figures in 1971 (when 26% of one family households had 1–2 dependent children in a total of 18.6 million households) and 1981 (25% of 20.2 million households).

(b) Alan realised that both questions dealt with **percentage increases**. He noticed that **the decades were not sequential** and he **showed how the calculations were made** – an essential requirement of this paper.

(c) Alan got no marks for this answer. He needed to say that there is **an absolute increase in the number of households** (1 mark) but that **the rate of increase is not consistent – lower during 1981–1991 than 1961–1971** (1 mark).

Don't forget ...

Take care when reading questions with figures. Use a ruler to work down each row if necessary.

Bring a calculator for exam papers that allow their use – and **know how to use it**.

Always show the working that leads to your answer.

Always check the marks available – if there are 2 marks in calculation questions you may need to make 2 points.

Question type 14

Look carefully at the table that follows. It gives information relating to problems which commuters face on a daily basis, showing the percentage of trains more than five minutes late. Having studied the table, answer the following question.

Why might the figures in the table give cause for concern?   [4 marks]

Trains more than five minutes late

Operators serving London area	September 1999 %	September 1998 %
Chiltern	6.6	12.8
Connex South Central	9.8	8.5
Connex South East	10.9	6.3
Gatwick Express	13.6	13.6
Great Eastern	6.1	6.7
LTS Rail	8.4	4.3
Silverlink	10.6	11.3
South West Trains	9.8	11.0
Thames Trains	7.9	11.4
Thameslink	11.0	6.4
WAGN	7.4	4.6

Source: *Statistics from the Shadow Strategic Rail Authority*

GEMMA'S ANSWER

According to the table there has been no real improvement for the London commuters. Although there is no consistent trend, things have got worse for some commuters. This can have an adverse impact on people going to work making them late or more stressed.

(3/4)

How to score full marks

Gemma has written a fairly effective answer. She started by **mentioning the table** and then made two points about the **lack of real improvements for commuters** and the fact that, for some, **the situation had worsened.** Gemma then made the point about the **possible impact** on those whose trains were regularly delayed.

She might have strengthened her answer by **including an example** of an improving service (Chiltern) and a deteriorating one (LTS Rail).

For a fourth mark, Gemma could have **considered the wider issue** of government policy and growing public concern/criticism.

Don't forget ...

Keep your answer fairly short if only a few marks are available.

Use examples from tables to support/amplify ideas where appropriate.

DATA SET AND COMPREHENSION QUESTIONS

Read the following information and answer the questions which follow.

Britons now spend more on fun than on any other household expenditure, as spending on leisure outstrips that on housing and food for the average family for the first time. Spending on holidays, home computers, sporting goods and other leisure goods and services now forms the largest share of household outgoings according to official figures.

Spending on leisure has risen from 9% of total outgoings 30 years ago to 17% in 1998–99, with the biggest rise in leisure services, such as sporting events, cable television, holidays and gambling. The average household now spends £16.20 a week on holidays, while those in London and the south east spend 25% more. These now account for 71% of all leisure spending. The 1998–99 family expenditure survey reveals that weekly spending varies hugely across the social spectrum, ranging from £110 for households in the lowest 10% of income groups to £770 in the highest. The average gross weekly income rose to £460, up £40 on the year before, after allowing for inflation.

Spending on electronic products such as television, videos, computers and audio equipment has quadrupled in the past 30 years, reaching £8 a week, on average, in 1998. Over the same period, food spending fell from 26% of total expenditure to 17%. Expenditure on mobile phones also rose in 1999, up by 25% on the previous year. Computers accounted for 31% of all purchases of electronic equipment in 1999. However, access to home computers varies hugely according to income group, with only 10% of low income households owning a computer, compared to 70% of high income families.'

5

10

15

Adapted from Julia Hartley-Brewer,
'Fun-loving Britons splash out most on leisure',
The Guardian, 25 November 1999.

Question types 12 and 6

(a) What is the annual expenditure of the average household on holidays? [3 marks]

(b) What was the average weekly spending on electronic products in 1968? [3 marks]

Explain briefly the meaning of each of the following, giving examples where appropriate:

(c) 'official figures' (line 4). [3 marks]

(d) 'across the social spectrum' (line 9). [3 marks]

SURJIT'S ANSWERS

(a) £16.20 x 52 weeks = £832   (1/3)

(b) 25% of £8 = £2   (3/3)

(c) These are officially approved by the government   (2/3)

(d) Covering a wide range.   (1/3)

How to score full marks

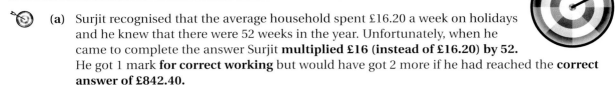

(a) Surjit recognised that the average household spent £16.20 a week on holidays and he knew that there were 52 weeks in the year. Unfortunately, when he came to complete the answer Surjit **multiplied £16 (instead of £16.20) by 52.** He got 1 mark **for correct working** but would have got 2 more if he had reached the **correct answer of £842.40.**

(b) Surjit **picked up the correct clues from the passage.** Lines 14–15 stated that 'spending on electronic products . . . has quadrupled . . . reaching £8 per week . . . in 1998'. After this, the 25% of £8 was straightforward.

(c) Surjit received 2 marks for a clear statement relating to **official government approval.** To receive a third mark, Surjit needed to say what 'These . . .' were. **Statistics, surveys and data** are examples of words that would have got him an extra mark.

(d) The final answer was **much too vague.** Surjit needed to **state clearly** that the 'social spectrum' meant **across social classes/different groups in society** to gain the other two marks.

Don't forget ...

Check calculations carefully to **minimise avoidable errors.**

Work carefully and methodically. It's easy to mis-read a figure – and simple mistakes quickly cost marks.

Try to make your answers **fully explicit.** Vague sentences win few marks.

Scan all the material on the question paper, including the rubric and instructions to candidates. Scanning gives you an idea of the overall content and shape of the questions.

Look critically at any information you are given. Figures are not necessarily always reliable. Check their source.

Read through any passages and tables of statistics carefully, making sure you understand what the questions require. Know how to use your calculator.

Show your working for calculations.

Move on if you get stuck, but return to the question at the end.

Don't panic at the sight of statistical tables. Look out for them in advance in newspapers, books and the internet. Familiarise yourself with the way statistics relating to society, politics and economics are presented.

Answer all questions. Marks are not deducted for incorrect answers.

Read this source on the subject of the monarchy in the United Kingdom and answer the question that follows.

THE MONARCHY

- Britain is a hereditary but constitutional monarchy.
- The Queen is head of state, but her role is largely ceremonial.
- The monarch is expected to remain politically impartial.
- The monarch can do no wrong as long as she acts on the advice of a responsible government with a majority in the House of Commons.

Functions

1 a symbol of continuity of the state and constitution
2 a symbol of national unity
3 the formal head of state.

Royal prerogative

Traditional powers of the monarch which, by convention, are now exercised by ministers of the Crown (usually the Prime Minister) and which do not require authorisation by Parliament e.g. dissolving and summoning Parliament, declaring war, making treaties.

Source: Dennis Kavanagh *British Politics* OUP 1996

Question types 5, 6

What is the role of the monarch in the United Kingdom according to this source?   [5 marks]

EMILY'S ANSWER

The Queen has the title of head of state but her role is mainly ceremonial. She does not lean towards any of the political parties. She is often seen as a symbol and may be an important figure in times of crisis because she stands for national unity.

An example of this was when the Queen's mother died recently and there was great national mourning. Many stood in freezing temperatures to file past the coffin and millions watched the funeral on television. This was an example of the royal family and national unity. The Queen mother had done the same in World War II.

(3/5)

How to score full marks

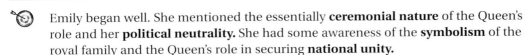

Emily began well. She mentioned the essentially **ceremonial nature** of the Queen's role and her **political neutrality.** She had some awareness of the **symbolism** of the royal family and the Queen's role in securing **national unity.**

Unfortunately, Emily received no marks for the second paragraph because it was entirely irrelevant. The question specifically stated that interpretations of the role of the monarch should be **according to this source.** Most of Emily's material in the second paragraph was gathered several years after the source was written.

Emily could have used the second paragraph to gain two extra marks. She might have mentioned the need for the Queen to act, when she is called upon to do so, **on the advice of a majority government.** To emphasise the limitations of the Queen's role, Emily could have referred to the way in which the traditional powers of **royal prerogative** had increasingly been **exercised by politicians**, especially the Prime Minister.

Don't forget ...

Make your answers match the marks available. Don't write long paragraphs if only three or four marks are available. If you do, you will not have enough time to complete the longer answers required later in the paper.

Use clear sentences to make your points. Don't leave the examiner to guess or interpret what you are trying to say. **Try to avoid using irrelevant material**. You will not lose marks for this, but it is time, and the chance to gain extra marks, wasted.

AQA Specification A Unit 3 requires skills that reflect the ability to look critically at a piece of source material in a way that will identify and explain its strengths and weaknesses.

Here is a typical example of such a question.

Question types 6, 8, 10

Read these two sources on the subject of the monarchy in the UK. Answer the question which follows:

What are the strengths and weaknesses of each of these sources?   [10 marks]

First source

In the first year of the third millennium, Britain still selects its head of state by her birth certificate. Are we content with the prospect of having a hereditary monarchy in another 100 years' time? This is not a question that politicians want to address. The ludicrous recent furore when Mo Mowlam mildly wondered whether the Windsors might move into a more modern home is testimony to the neurosis among politicians about any discussion of becoming a republic.

Unlike nearly every other democracy in the world, the British constitution treats us as subjects, not as free, equal and sovereign citizens. Well, who cares? Don't we all know it is a fiction?

The Queen reigns: the Prime Minister rules. The powers are in her name, but they are really wielded by Number 10. Her honours list and her bishops are selected in Downing Street. The monarchy is just a glittering delivery carriage for the decisions of the Government.

The monarchy remains symbolic of privilege over people, of chance over endeavour, of being something rather than doing something. We elevate to the apex of our society someone selected not on the basis of talent or achievement, but because of genes. For all the lip-service that politicians of all parties pay to meritocracy, for so long as we have a hereditary monarchy, Britain enthrones and glorifies the exact opposite.

Source: Editorial *The Observer* 30 July 2000

Second source

I have read *The Observer* uninterrupted for the best part of 40 years. That relationship is in severe jeopardy if there are any more editorials of the ilk of last Sunday and hatchet jobs on the Royal Family as you had the temerity to perpetrate upon Her Majesty Queen Elizabeth, the Queen Mother, a fortnight ago. And I cannot be alone in this view.

If the United Kingdom were to become a presidency next year, the incumbent would be a politician. Which of the current bunch do you suggest would make a suitable president? Better the devil you know than the one who is elected because he or she has the most money to spend! I rest my case. Let us have no more of this unutterable nonsense.

Source: Reader's letter to *The Observer* in response to its editorial and earlier article on the Queen Mother, *The Observer* 6 August 2000.

JAMIE'S ANSWER

One of the main problems with both of the sources is that they are biased. The first source comes from a broadsheet newspaper, which makes it more reliable but an editorial should be more neutral.

A strength of the first source is the way it uses language to persuade the reader. It says that Britain still selects its head of state by birth certificate and that, unlike nearly every other democracy in the world, we are treated as subjects not free and equal citizens. Really the Minister rules so there is not much point in having a monarchy if it is only a glittering delivery carriage for the decisions of Tony Blair. This source is very strong on rhetoric.

The second source is biased from another direction. The reader shows a lot of emotion and this is a weakness. He states that he is not alone in his view about the newspaper and the way it has criticised the Queen Mother.

This source points out the dangers of having a president instead of a queen. The reader proves that having a republic would mean having a president who is elected because he is rich. This would be no better than having someone who happens to be born into the right family. It is unutterable nonsense.

On the other hand this could be seen as a very old-fashioned view from someone who must be old if he has read The Observer uninterrupted for 40 years. Also we don't know who really wrote the letter because it doesn't give the reader's name. (5/10)

How to score full marks

- Jamie scores a mark in the first sentence by stating that both sources are **biased**. In his second sentence he might have said that **broadsheet newspapers are more reliable than tabloids** and he could also have made the point that *The Observer* traditionally takes a **left-of-centre** political position which is not always sympathetic to the concept of monarchy.

- In the second paragraph there is a good point about **persuasive language** but, instead of giving examples like '. . . a glittering delivery carriage for the decisions of Government', Jamie starts to summarise the text and gains no marks for much of this paragraph. He closes by mentioning **rhetoric** but again fails to provide examples or to show in what ways rhetoric might be both a strength *and* a weakness.

- Jamie uses both sources, as the question requires, and gains a mark in the third paragraph for stating that **emotional writing** ('let us have no more of this unutterable nonsense') can be seen as a weakness. However, he fails to build on this in the next sentence, which merely restates something said in the source.

- Jamie's fourth paragraph is muddled and he should not try to argue that the reader has **proved** his case on the basis of the evidence in the source. Jamie's closing paragraph doesn't really offer a conclusion but he **could be correct in implying that support for the monarchy is not as strong as it was**. Similarly the **anonymity** of the letter might be a potential weakness.

- Overall, Jamie's answer lacked consistency. He needed **to illustrate his points by using supporting examples from the sources.** Strengths and weaknesses needed to be **more clearly identified** (e.g. both sources are weak because they are one-sided and lack evidence) and he needed **to avoid summarising bits of the source.** More **critical evaluation of the arguments** and **distinguishing between fact and opinion** would have raised his mark.

Look critically at all material presented to you. Statistics in social sciences are not automatically 'facts'. Nor are words.

Interpretation can be crucial. Statistics might be entirely reliable but they are often **interpreted** by people whose views are less than objective. (Opinion polls often fall into this category.)

Newspapers, magazines and books contain a **mixture of fact and opinion.** Broadsheet newspapers are often biased, although the bias is rather less obvious than in other papers such as the tabloids.

Don't dismiss the tabloids. They are often well written and informative – and they reach a large audience.

All newspapers have a political stance (and so do many writers). Find out about the political stance of the major national daily and Sunday papers.

Don't try to learn masses of information about different subjects. General Studies covers a very wide area even within one of the three AS Units. It is far more important to **develop and practise skills** of analysis and evaluation.

Read sources with care. Figures in particular can easily be mis-read.

If a question is based on two sources, make sure your answer covers both.

Always try to focus on the question set. Write in **clear and specific terms** instead of making sweeping statements and wild generalisations.

Make sure your answers always identify strengths and weaknesses of sources. Don't write lengthy summaries of the sources where the occasional strength and weakness **will be lost in a mass of detail.**

Remember to be critical, but in a positive way. The examiner is unlikely to support all the views expressed in the sources he uses. Don't be afraid to express a criticism **but do so constructively and use evidence to back up the view expressed.**

There are four assessment objectives in General Studies (see also page 7) and these are reflected in marks for individual questions. In summary form these are:

● Assessment Objective 1 (AO1): knowledge and understanding
● Assessment Objective 2 (AO2): clear and accurate communication
● Assessment Objective 3 (AO3): concepts, data use, selecting & using evidence, interpretation, evaluation
● Assessment Objective 4 (AO4): demonstrating an understanding of different types of knowledge, the relationship between them and appreciating their limitations.

So far, in short-answer questions, marks have been given to candidates who can meet AO1 and AO3. The question on page 65, on the strengths and weaknesses of two sources about the monarchy, had 10 marks which were divided up like this:

● AO2 = 2 marks
● AO3 = 4 marks
● AO4 = 4 marks

Jamie was not very successful in the quest for AO4 marks – and most AS candidates find themselves in the same position. The two questions/answers that follow focus on questions in which up to 15 marks are available, some of which are for AO4 skills and content.

Read the following article and answer the two questions which follow.

Should prisoners be allowed TV sets in their cells?

This article is based on a series of letters printed in The Guardian, *in which Fran Russell of the Howard league for Penal Reform argued the case in favour of the Prison Service proposals.*

The Prison Service has announced a plan to put many more television sets in prison cells. It is a very positive move. Resettlement in the community after a prison sentence is more likely to be successful if a person has kept in touch with the outside world.

People sentenced to imprisonment lose their liberty, not their rights as human beings, as citizens – and freedom of information is an important right which access to television can   5
help to satisfy. It can be used as a useful incentive in encouraging co-operation and good behaviour, which can make life easier for all those serving sentences, as well as for prison staff. It could also be a useful tool in widening opportunities for education, crucial to rehabilitation.

Prisoners are locked in their cells for a minimum of 15 hours a day; many for up to 23   10
hours. It is during that time that suicides are attempted and many men, women and children in prison are driven to mutilate themselves. I believe it is the punitive culture and ethos of prison that leads many of these people to violence. Suicides, now at record levels, as well as self-mutilation, fights and attacks on staff could all be reduced by television in cells, since it can lessen the sense of isolation. A more peaceful environment can be created for staff and   15

prisoners.

Television is an intrinsic part of our culture – by giving people access to the outside world, it can remove them, albeit for a short time, from the brutal environment in which they are placed – especially if rehabilitation not retribution is our aim. 20

I know it will be said that overcrowding and lack of resources are the fundamental problems in our prisons, but I do not believe that funds for televisions would have much long-term impact on improving regimes. Conditions in many prisons are so bad as to be morally reprehensible, so bad that it might be argued we are denying prisoners essential human rights. Televisions will not solve those problems, but they might help 25 improve, a little, the emotional well-being of people locked alone in their cells isolated from the world.

Source: adapted from *The Guardian*, 5 June 1999

Question type 9

(a) Name **three** different types of knowledge used in the passage and give an example of each type.

[6 marks]

Question type 8, 11

(b) What is Fran Russell's conclusion? To what extent is her conclusion justified by the arguments she uses in the passage?

[4 marks]

There will be an additional 3 marks for quality of written communication.

TAYA'S ANSWER

(a) There are different kinds of knowledge. One type of knowledge is the one which is based on belief. An example comes in the second sentence which says 'It is a very positive move.' This shows a belief that the move to put more television sets in cells was worthwhile.

As well as beliefs there are facts. We are told that prisoners are locked in their cells for long periods, nearly 24 hours a day for some.

Altogether there are a number of examples of different types of knowledge throughout this interesting article which shows that the author, Fran Russell, is very well informed about how to reform prisons. 3/6

(b) I agree with Fran Russell's conclusion that it would be more humane to allow prisoners who have little contact with others to have television sets in their cells. She makes several points to support this sort of approach which is why she is connected with the Howard League for Penal Reform. 1/4

How to score full marks

The mark allocation for this question is as follows:

- AO2 = 3 marks
- AO4 = 10 marks

(a) Taya has some understanding of the concept of different types of knowledge and gains two marks for her first paragraph for including the idea of **knowledge related to belief** together with a supporting example.

Taya's second paragraph is less explicit. Knowledge based on **fact** is likely to be related to **secure evidence** and an approach that might require **objectivity.** She needed to make this clear in the example she chose.

In her third paragraph, Taya could have gained two further marks by writing about **subjective knowledge**, perhaps using Fran Russell's comment that 'I believe it is a punitive culture and ethos of prison that leads many of these people to violence.'

Other forms of knowledge which Taya might have used are **truth, falsity, scientific** and **moral.**

In questions like this one, 1 mark would be awarded for each **type of knowledge**, with a second mark for each **example from the article.**

(b) Taya just manages to get a mark. She has a vague awareness that a conclusion is something that must be **consistent with the evidence**. Taya also needs to be aware that **interpretation of the evidence** may make it possible to reach **several different conclusions.** Consequently, to secure all three marks in this section, Taya needed to **summarise the main points** made by the author and then **make her own judgment** on their quality.

Taya scored 2/3 marks for communication. The extra mark would have been given for **more confident and informed writing** about, perhaps capturing the difference between those who see prison as places for punishment and those, like Fran Russell, who stress the need for rehabilitation of prisoners to reduce the chance of re-offending.

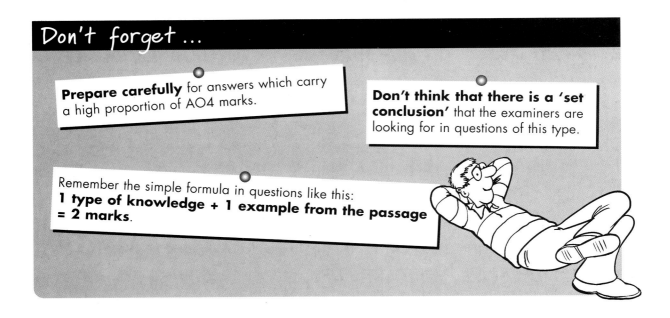

Don't forget ...

Prepare carefully for answers which carry a high proportion of AO4 marks.

Don't think that there is a 'set conclusion' that the examiners are looking for in questions of this type.

Remember the simple formula in questions like this:
1 type of knowledge + 1 example from the passage = 2 marks.

2   Read this source and answer the question that follows.

> It is very hard for the political nation in Britain to discuss the monarchy in sensible terms. By most people and for much of the time it is accepted as simply being there, somewhat like the weather: rather baffling but a fixture and very much part of the scene, part of the specialness of being British and often a source of self-congratulation verging on the smug. A decade ago, the journalist Sir Peregrine Worthsthorne could declare: 'These days the only efficient part of the British Constitution is the Monarchy' without raising a ripple of dissent from his audience of political scientists. A few months earlier, in July 1984, the historian Lord Blake said:
>
> > 'No doubt the preservation of the monarchy, like that of liberty, requires eternal vigilance, but I see no reasons whatever to believe that this will be kept any less in the future than it has been in the past.'
>
> > Ten years on, thanks chiefly to the personal misfortunes of some members of the Royal Family, waves of heated speculation about the durability of the House of Windsor afflicted the press.'

Source: Peter Hennessy, *The Hidden Wiring*, (Indigo), 1996

Peter Hennessy states that 'It is very hard for the political nation in Britain to discuss the monarchy in sensible terms.'

What is he likely to mean by this sentence? Why do you think it is so difficult for the nation to have a sensible discussion about the monarchy?   [15 marks]

This is an excellent opening. It recognises that the question is in two parts and that the first part needs a relatively short response. Tom recognises the extent to which there is no quick way of deciding what the author means but two viable alternatives are mentioned.

This is an effective second paragraph, which indicates the boundaries of what we might be able to prove and implying that it might be decided on personal beliefs or values.

TOM'S ANSWER

In the first part of the question, Peter Hennessy asks what is likely to be meant by 'the political nation'. He offers no clues so in some respects it is a matter of interpretation. It could mean everyone who is entitled to vote or it could mean those who are more informed and who involve themselves more in the political process.

One of the main reasons why it is difficult to have a sensible discussion about the monarchy is that the subject is controversial. Some people support the idea of a monarchy but others are opposed to it and favour a republic. It is not possible to prove, one way or the other, which is the best form of government.

Another interesting point and one which is valid. Tom might, though, have gone on to try to identify some of the criteria of a sensible argument.

Another reason is that people get emotional about the monarchy. This was seen at the time of the death of Princess Diana when there was a great outpouring of national grief. In contrast, those who are critical of the monarchy are also very fixed in their beliefs. This is not the way to have a sensible argument.

The recognition that knowledge is not fixed and that attitudes can change over time is very important as an AO4 point.

The fact that views can change over time is reflected in the source when the author takes the time frame beyond that of Sir Peregrine Worthsthorne and Lord Blake. Knowledge is not always fixed and attitudes can change.

What a pity that Tom did not take the point about making an objective judgment further. He might also have explored how we acquire knowledge.

Taking this further, there is evidence to support the last sentence. The activities of the Royal Family are widely reported, especially by the tabloids. In recent times, there have been divorces and other events which do not always portray members of the Royal Family in a very flattering light. How are people meant to make an objective judgment?

Tom seeks to reach a conclusion which is well supported. He calls for rationality and suggests that most people are likely to express an opinion which is not formed by a careful or wide consideration of the evidence.

Most people probably aren't really bothered one way or the other about the monarchy. It is there and is a part of our history. If anyone is going to have a sensible discussion they need to do so in a way that is rational, calm and informed.. The monarchy is a very subjective thing and most people simply aren't very well informed.

13/15

How to score full marks

 The mark allocation for this questions is as follows:
- AO2 = 4 marks
- AO3 = 3 marks
- AO4 = 8 marks

 Questions sometimes come in two parts with the first as a brief 'lead in'. Make sure you answer both – as Tom did.

Particularly where there are more than five marks available, questions are marked in bands with criteria, which answers must reflect. Here, Tom reached the top band with the criteria that: answers should be **well ordered**, with **sustained** and **logical critical evaluation** of how a discussion 'in sensible terms' might be carried out with **clear and sustained ability** to **examine** and **analyse** the factors that might inhibit this. These are some of the **skills** which you need to demonstrate to reach the highest mark bands.

 Examiners are not looking for the perfect answer. Tom did not, in the early part of his answer, expand his thoughts on the **criteria for a sensible discussion** but he did so in a very effective **conclusion** when he mentioned that such a decision should be **rational, calm and informed,** contrasting this with most discussions about the monarchy which tend to be **subjective.** Writing a **conclusion** is a very important part of the answer.

 An extra two marks would have come in the last but one paragraph, which Tom closed by posing a question about making an **objective judgment. Beware of too much rhetoric.**

Question types 3, 7, 8, 11

'People with plenty of leisure time don't have sufficient money to enjoy it.'

Critically examine arguments for and against this view. [17 marks]

There will be an additional 3 marks for quality of written communication.

AMANDA'S ANSWER

A rather fragmented start, which only addresses the question in a limited way.

It all depends on why you have plenty of time. Some people have more time because they have retired. Some people have more time even if they do'nt want it. Among these are the unemployed. If they have no reglar wage they have to rely on the dole so they don't have much money.

Amanda is describing the situation instead of looking critically at the arguments.

One of the problems with leisure is the cost although it depends what you do. There is a great boom in gyms and fitness centres but a lot of these are expensive. Even going to football is expensive if you support one of the top teams..

A fair point – there is far more early retirement and not all leisure is expensive.

It is more common these days for people to retire early but they may not have much money though they have plenty of time and may want to take up new interests. Not all leisure is expensive. You can join a library or go to an evening class to follow new things. These are cheap. You can keep fit by jogging and the swimming baths have cheap sessions. Old people get bus passes.

Amanda is generalising and going off the point. Spelling errors continue.

Sometimes it seems that leisure is for young people who are fit and energetic. Lots of people go to the club scene but that would cost too much for retured people even if they were intrested (which they wont be). Young people have more money to spend but if they don't they can hang out with there mates.

Limited and superficial conclusion.

Often young people have plenty of leisure time after school if their not doing a part-time job. If they do they can enjoy their leisure time though it doe'snt always take money to do it. That could be true for others as well.

4+1=5/20

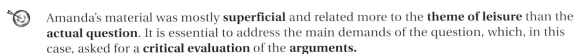

The mark allocation for this question is as follows:
- AO2 = 3 marks
- AO3 = 17 marks

Amanda's material was mostly **superficial** and related more to the **theme of leisure** than the **actual question**. It is essential to address the main demands of the question, which, in this case, asked for a **critical evaluation** of the **arguments.**

Amanda needed to pay more attention to **spelling** and her **style** was sometimes rather personalised. ('It all depends on why *you* have plenty of time.')

The first paragraph had some ideas about leisure connected with **retirement** or **unemployment** but they were not **clearly expressed.** Amanda might have gained more marks by dealing with the two **separately.**

The second paragraph started quite well (cost of leisure) but the idea was **not effectively developed. Clearer and more detailed examples** were needed.

Amanda made quite a good point (**trend towards early retirement**) at the start of the third paragraph and this middle section was the strongest part of her answer. She indicated that **not all leisure need be expensive** and she supported this with **relevant examples.**

The concluding paragraphs were far less successful, especially with **the assumption that most people who were not young were bound to have dull and sedentary interests.**

Amanda could have included the **high spending power of young consumers** to make a contrast with other groups – including those who retire early with fairly generous pensions and who **can afford a range of potentially new leisure pursuits**.

Amanda made some attempt to provide a conclusion and there was a hint of the sort of **critical evaluation of arguments** that should have been the **essential thread running through the answer.** Not all leisure pursuits undertaken by young people are expensive but Amanda needed **examples** of both this and the extent to which this **might not be true for others as well.**

One additional mark was added for communication that **uses a form and style of writing appropriate to purpose and subject matter.**

Don't forget ...

Try to avoid **too much descriptive writing** when the question asks for **critical evaluation of arguments.**

Aim to make your answer **as coherent as possible** with paragraphs that follow each other **in a natural sequence. Use a new paragraph for each idea but try to link them.**

Draw together your thoughts and ideas **to form a conclusion.**

The OCR Unit 3 Social Domain examination involves the completion of an essay that carries 50 marks. This is an example:

Question types 3, 7, 8, 11

More people are finding that some form of work experience is a good preparation for work although there are others who take a different view.

(a) Explain clearly the difference between work and work experience. [10 marks]

(b) Identify and discuss the factors which are seen to contribute to 'good' and 'bad' work experience. [40 marks]

DARREN'S ANSWER

> **No problems here – a full range of points clearly noting the essential differences.**

One of the most obvious differences between work and work experience is that you get paid for the former but not for the latter. Most schools now have a scheme of work experience in Yr 10 or Yr 11 and this leads to another difference. Work experience is like a 'taste' of real work but only for a shot time, (a week or two) not like most jobs. People who work usually have a contract but this does not apply to work experience people from school. On work experience you have a bit more freedom. Real workers usually have to follow stricter rules. The last difference is that work comes in different forms e.g. part-time but in work experience you go for the whole work or fortnight.

(10/10)

> **A lengthy opening but too much detail. Only the final sentence is relevant to the question.**

I have recently finished my work experience. All Yr11's have to do work experience and it takes place after the mock GCSE exams in December. An interesting feature is that we have to arrange our own work experience although it is checked out by the Careers teachers. It lasts for two weeks and you can have two weeks in one placement or a week in two. This is a good idea if you are undecided about the sort of job you want.

> **Darren is describing the start of his work experience when he should be evaluating it.**

As I have a fairly clear idea about what I want to do (a solicitor) I did two weeks in a local firm. This meant making sure that I was smartly dressed and punctual. It also meant overcoming my nerves as there is a big difference between school and work. (The latter seems much more grown up.)

At first I didn't really know anyone but people made me very welcome and I quickly felt at home so I would say that this was a good thing. Among the things I did during the first week was making the coffee, sorting out stock and photocopying. I didn't really get to learn much about being a solicitor, which was a bad thing.

The second week was better and I was allowed to look at law books and go on the Internet (where I found some interesting staff e-mails that the school might not have been very pleased about). By the end of the work experience I knew a bit more about being a solicitor which is a good thing. However, it was quite boring so I don't know if I really want to be a solicitor even though it seems to be well paid.

6/40

How to score full marks

The mark allocation for part **(a)** is as follows:
- AO1 = 4 marks
- AO2 = 2 marks
- AO3 = 4 marks

Darren did everything that was required to gain full marks for part (a). He made **a range of clear points** contrasting **the differences** between work and work experience with **plenty of examples.** It was **exactly the right length** for an 'introductory essay' worth only 10 of the 50 marks.

The mark allocation for part **(b)** is:
- AO1 = 10 marks
- AO2 = 7 marks
- AO3 = 14 marks
- AO4 = 9 marks

Most of the things Darren did in the 40-mark part of the essay were never likely to win him many marks. His account was **highly personalised** (a brief outline of his experiences) with just the occasional reference to something that he considered 'good' or 'bad'.

Darren needed to do what the question required – to **identify** and **discuss** the factors which would allow him to make an **informed evaluation** of his work experience.

To gain AO4 marks, Darren needed to establish **criteria** on which to make judgments about whether his work experience was **'good'** or **'bad'** – expectations set against experience, skills acquired, inter-personal relations, knowledge about procedures, satisfaction, preparation for a more extended period of placement, etc.

Not all students will agree about what might constitute a 'good or 'bad' work experience and Darren needed to state this. With that qualification, among **'good'** experiences, Darren might have mentioned some of the following:

- the opportunity to practise skills
- scope to adapt behaviour to requirements of the work environment
- the extent to which he met the needs of the providers of the work experience
- variety of tasks
- specialist experience
- organisation
- appropriateness of the working environment
- the extent to which the student/provider were clear about the aims of the placement.

Darren mentioned only in passing **the welcome** and the **greater variety of tasks** during the second week.

 'Bad' experiences might have included:

- poor structure
- the lack of relevance
- poor working conditions
- lack of communication
- exploitation
- inadequate supervision.

Again, in passing, Darren made oblique references to **lack of relevance** during the first week and **boredom.**

 Darren's conclusion needed to be based on a **balance** between 'good' and 'bad' points.

Don't forget ...

Don't describe when you should be **discussing** and **evaluating.**

Always use **continuous prose** rather than **bullet points** in an essay.

Make sure your answer for 40 marks is **demonstrably longer** than the part of the question that is worth only 10 marks.

You have to satisfy all four assessment objectives:
- balance **content** with **concepts** and always put the emphasis on **analysis and evaluation** rather than description.

Make sure your points are **clearly communicated.**

QUESTIONS TO TRY

SHORT-ANSWER COMPREHENSION QUESTIONS

Question type 6

1 Read the following information and answer the questions based on it.

'Despite being more indebted than ever, consumers last year showed a greater inclination to spend than save. The 16th Annual British Lifestyles Survey published by the market researchers Mintel examines consumer trends and opinions. The report says that the ageing population will cause dramatic changes in consumer habits, but shoppers are more discerning   5
and expect increased competition to work in their favour. The next five years will see the 'grey pound' becoming more important.

'The internet and other new technologies will become crucial,' said Paul Rickard, head of research at Mintel. 'In terms of total consumer spending the web will have an impact on prices. The service industries will   10
be forced into higher productivity thanks to the internet. The web will create consortia of buyers who will drive prices down: the balance of power will fall more and more with the consumer'.

The top lifestyle priority for most people, however, remains home ownership, with 63% rating it as their most important asset. The south-east   15
property boom has fuelled a 26% rise in prices since 1989. Spending on services such as domestic and garden help has grown by 45% in a decade. Convenience foods rose by 16% to 1994 and by a further 17% since. They are particularly important to 15–24 year-olds and 'sedentary' females.'

**Source: Adapted from *Wiser, older shoppers ready to splash out* by Paul Kelso,
The Guardian 9 February 2000.**

Explain briefly the meaning of each of the following, giving examples where appropriate.

(a) 'consumer trends' (lines 3–4).   [3 marks]

(b) 'the grey pound' (line 7).   [3 marks]

(c) 'The service industries will be forced into higher productivity thanks to the internet.' (lines 10–11).   [3 marks]

(d) 'Convenience foods . . . are particularly important to 15–24 year-olds and sedentary females' (lines 18–19).   [3 marks]

2 Look at the table and answer the questions that follow. **Calculators may be used.**

Population by gender and age for the United Kingdom

Ages	%Under 16	% aged 16–64	% aged 65 and over	All ages (= 100%) (millions)
Males				
1931	25.6	67.7	6.7	22.1
1961	24.8	65.8	9.4	25.5
1991	21.4	65.8	12.8	28.2
1998	21.3	65.5	13.2	29.1
Females				
1931	23.0	68.9	8.1	24.0
1961	22.1	63.9	14.0	27.3
1991	19.3	62.1	18.5	29.6
1998	19.6	62.2	18.2	30.1

Source: *Office for National Statistics.* Crown copyright 1999.

Question types 1, 12

(a) What was the total number of men and women aged over 65 in 1999? [1 mark]

    A 902,256   **C** 9,021,650   **E** 9,108,960

    B 912,560   **D** 9,085,600

Question type 14

(b) Comment on the trends shown in the proportions of the male population of the UK between 1931 and 1998. [3 marks]

DATA INTERPRETATION QUESTIONS

Question type 15

3 Look carefully at the table and answer the question that follows. The table gives information relating to problems which commuters face on a daily basis. It shows the percentage of passengers in excess of capacity during the morning and evening rush hours.

(Passenger totals in brackets)	Autumn 1998 (%)	Autumn 1997 (%)
Chiltern	0.5 (12 005)	2.0 (12 693)
Connex South Central	2.9 (122 705)	4.8 (118 575)
Connex South East	1.8 (214 731)	3.0 (214 548)
Great Eastern	2.7 (91 816)	3.3 (91 042)
LTS Rail	0.6 (49 408)	1.4 (44 405)
Silverlink	2.7 (30 812)	1.9 (30 913)
South West Trains	3.9 (137 954)	3.8 (129 218)
Thames Trains	2.6 (18 481)	2.1 (17 312)
Thameslink	7.1 (52 181)	4.4 (48 691)
WAGN	1.2 (84 125)	0.6 (81 269)

Source: *Statistics from Shadow Strategic Rail Authority*

Why might the information in this table be of limited value? [8 marks]

Question types 6, 8, 10

4   Read this source on the subject of race relations. Answer the question that follows.

Britain is foul, racist and deeply prejudiced. The evidence is overwhelming. For every high profile racist attack, there are hundreds of others – some reported, some not. For every physical attack, there are a thousand verbal assaults. Underpinning it all is an insidious, systematic racism that subtly and not so subtly discriminates against black people from cradle to grave. The conventional white wisdom is that racial issues have vastly improved.

After 15 years in a mixed marriage this is the first time I have written about my personal experiences. I do so now reluctantly, only to add my voice to others trying to shake up a complacent liberal intelligentsia and an establishment that parrots platitudes and accepts that things are generally fine. An establishment that mouths sorrow following the Lawrence case and that is as guilty as the foul-mouthed, Union Jack-clad yob on the street corner who stuffs British National Party leaflets into letterboxes and beats up vulnerable black people for fun.

**Source: adapted from Richard Ellis, *Race hate in Britain is rife – just ask my wife*,
The Observer, 26 March 2000.**

What are the strengths and weaknesses of this source when assessing the extent
of the problem of racism?   [10 marks]

LONGER COMPREHENSION QUESTIONS WITH AO4

Question types 8, 9, 10, 11

5   'The absence of certain knowledge makes it difficult to convince the public of the need for anti-pollution policies.'

How far do you agree with this statement?   [10 marks]

6   Read these two sources on the subject of drugs, politics and the law. Answer the question which follows.

First source
The Tories announced their new drugs policy yesterday. There can hardly be a person under 50 who will not read their new proposals with incredulity: possession of drugs within 400 metres of a school would lead to a prison sentence. Anyone supplying a Class A drug (including ecstasy) to a minor for a second time would receive a life sentence. Supplying a Class B drug (cannabis) for the third time would get a seven-year sentence. William Hague says: 'A Conservative government will move in the opposite direction. Not more tolerance of drugs but less. Not softer policing, but tougher enforcement. Not making excuses but locking up offenders.'

This is crude spin at its most despicable. This is government not by what works, but by what the papers say. Time and again whenever anyone in power who actually knows anything about drugs dares to tell the truth that is blindingly obvious, all politicians feel obliged to step out and lie brazenly. They say what they quite plainly cannot believe and then they call for focus groups to find out why the young and a growing number of others so despise politics and politicians that they no longer bother to vote.

Source: Polly Toynbee, *Mo and the Drugs Tsar Both Tell the Truth. Others Don't,* *The Guardian*, 9 February 2000.

Second source

I think its time that people faced up to the truth about drugs instead of hiding behind words like 'recreational' and 'soft'. The reality is that *all* drugs are harmful and condemn users to a life of misery. This is what doctors will tell you. Drugs breed dependency and dependency leads to crime. This is the truth. Only the journalists in their nice London houses think that drugs are harmless. Not round here they're not. Not among the discarded needles, closed-up shops, kicked-in front doors and everyone on the dole. I've seen the effects on my own children and grandchildren.

What would I do? I'd have all the teenagers watching that film, *Trainspotting,* and all the journalists who want to legalise drugs can come and live on this estate for a fortnight. That would get them a bit closer to the truth.

Source: adapted from a letter to a local newspaper, 14 February 2000

Both sources claim to 'tell the truth' about the drugs situation. What arguments might be used to question whether either source is 'telling the truth'? [15 marks]

EXTENDED WRITING AND ESSAY-STYLE QUESTIONS

Question types 3, 7, 8, 11

These are set by **Edexcel** and **OCR.**

7 'There are no real differences between the three largest British political parties.' Critically examine arguments for and against this statement. [17 marks]

There will be an additional 3 marks for quality of written communication.

8 It is often said that some people who receive social benefits are 'scroungers' and that they should not be receiving such support because they do not need or deserve it.

What are social benefits? Give three examples to support your answer. [10 marks]

Discuss the attitude that those who receive social benefits are scroungers and that the system is regularly being cheated. How strong is the case for the continuing existence of the benefit system in the light of these arguments? [40 marks]

Answers can be found on pages 91–96.

1 Culture, morality, arts and humanities

Answers to multiple-choice questions (pages 27–28)

Question	Correct answer	Examiner's hints
1.	B	This question **tests your understanding of a common idiom**. A parapet is a protective wall or barrier that you find high up on a building, bridge or the like. To stick your head above it means that you reveal your position – literally to your enemy in a battle or (as in this case) figuratively on a contentious issue.
2.	D	This **follows up the first question** by asking about the origin of the expression. As parapet is associated with fortifications and defence, the answer is 'warfare'.
3.	A	The main point of this paragraph is that, **although the comedian appeared to be sending up his own race through the colour of his skin, his education and class meant that he was not**. Although the audience may not have understood this (D), the essential point is A.
4.	B	Although the author ends the paragraph by posing a question, which may point to answer D, the question is rhetorical – and **the answer 'no' is clearly implied** from what has gone before. This shows the author's 'disapproval'.
5.	D	**The 'context' is the circumstance surrounding or connected with something and is a word you should be familiar with**. All of the options could apply in theory, but you have to choose the best, which in this case is the most general, which is 'situation'.
6.	A	**'Irony' is another important word you should know for this unit**. Quite often, when you are being ironic you say the opposite of what you really mean. In the context of paragraph 10 and the discussion about race and humour, 'not intending seriously what you say' is the most appropriate response.
7.	B	In this type of question you have to decide whether both of the statements X and Y are correct, accurate or valid, and if they are whether statement Y follows from X. In paragraph 7 Jim Davidson is praised by the author for using material that many think is taboo (should be prohibited), so statement X is correct. The author also claims in paragraph 10 that all comedy should be judged on its merits, which corresponds to Y. But Y does not follow logically from X, as it is not the cause or consequence of X. **There is no direct link between the two statements**, leading to answer B.
8.	D	This type of question, like the previous one, is harder because **you have to go through several stages to arrive at the correct answer**. It also concerns the overall sense of the author's arguments in the passage and you have to **evaluate each statement in its own right**. You should allow for the possibility that none of the options could be correct (although this doesn't apply here), just one, some of them, or all of them. In this case they are all major points which the author argues in the passage about the BSC guideline. Point 1 is developed in paragraphs 3 and 4, point 2 is the concluding point made in the last sentence of paragraph 10, and point 3 is argued in paragraph 2.
9.	C	A 'conundrum' is a puzzle, a riddle, or even a dilemma – something where the answer is difficult to work out. All the options here are vaguely possible and once again you must **choose the one which fits best overall**. Essentially you will find the author's conclusion in the last sentence of the passage – that the relationship between race and comedy is complex and that it is difficult to decide what is acceptable.

10.   B   Here you have to **use your own judgement** about the author's
                arguments. He rejects the BSC guideline on racial humour and
                argues at the end of paragraph 9 that you can tell any kind of joke,
                provided that 'you do it in the right way', and (paragraph 10) 'with
                irony' – 'it all depends on the context', he says. However, this doesn't
                provide a very clear definition of what is, or is not, acceptable.

Answers to short-answer and essay questions (page 29)

🎯 How to score full marks

1.   Comedians and audiences face numerous problems in dealing with humour about
     race. These come from the difficulty in defining what is and is not acceptable and what
     society's response to it should be.

     The passage raises a number of different viewpoints about racial humour, from those
     who find it 'offensive and racist', to those who feel 'you can say anything as long as you
     do it in the right way'. This highlights the fact that the set values which we use to judge
     what is and is not acceptable vary widely from person to person and circumstance to
     circumstance. Paul Duddridge claims that the values or views of a working-class comic
     are not the same as 'the white chattering classes'. There is little or no consensus on the
     issue and this means that no firm standards or rules can be set.

     Whilst the article suggests that British comics would no longer do overtly racist
     humour, e.g. a white comic ridiculing black people, the author highlights the fact that
     comics continue to do routines that ridicule the same ethnic group, but come from an
     entirely different class and culture to the one they are making fun of. The author
     challenges the idea that this is more acceptable than the humour of comics such as
     Bernard Manning and gives the example of the university-educated comic doing a
     routine about American rap stars, where the audience assumed that he was ridiculing
     his own race. Comedy about race is not a simple issue as it encompasses ideas of class
     and culture also, and crossing these boundaries can cause just as much offence as the
     simple difference between black and white.

     Racial humour may also be judged on the way in which it is received, and by whom. In the
     passage Ollie Wilson makes the point that the BBC's *Goodness Gracious Me* is watched by
     white and middle-class audiences. The humour of the programme is based on 'ethnic
     minorities who are taking the rise out of their parents and communities'. Wilson asks
     whether it is right for white people to enjoy such derogatory humour, just because it is
     enacted by ethnic minorities, when it would probably not be acceptable if done by whites.

     On the other hand, many people argue the need for artistic freedom in comedy and
     that attempts to restrict racial humour intensify the taboo surrounding race. The
     article concludes that humour that is about race must be judged within a context and
     that people often instinctively know what is acceptable, regardless of any guidelines.

     > **Examiner's comments**
     >
     > This answer was awarded full marks because **it showed very good grasp of the key
     > issues for comedians *and* audiences and justified the points with appropriate
     > arguments, illustrations and references to the text.** The range of possible points were:
     >
     > ● issues are complex; some people want restraints, others want freedom
     > ● difficult to predict how an audience or individuals will react; people have
     >   different views about what is funny
     > ● may offend individuals with particular sensitivities; race (like religion) is a
     >   particularly sensitive matter for some
     > ● often involves sweeping generalisations and unfair stereotyping
     > ● sensitivities are not evenly distributed; seems OK to insult some nationalities,
     >   but not others
     > ● differences between skin colour and race/culture can be easily/conveniently blurred
     > ● difficult to know what lines should be drawn; impossible to devise appropriate rules.

> The candidate has covered most of these points, but not all were needed to score full marks. **What counts most is an overall sense of the issues and what the question is getting at, and the ability to support a good number of the arguments with appropriate references and illustrations.**
>
> One typical weakness in students' answers was **too much literal quotation from the text without necessarily explaining the point.**
>
> Some candidates who did not appreciate the difference between 'racial' and 'racist' often got into difficulties in terms of the meaning they wished to convey.
>
> **A student who is able to demonstrate that he or she can see the issues in the broader context** – such as preoccupation with 'political correctness', the inconsistencies, subjective elements, the more subtle points about who really sets the agenda in what might be judged acceptable, and the general impossibility of seeking to codify such matters – **will gain the highest marks.**

2. First and foremost, this statement by the author is a statement of belief and, as such, can only stand as an opinion which he argues. The starting point for the argument, however, is the BSC guideline that comedy about race should only be done by comedians poking fun at their own race, which the author regards as an inappropriate restriction, as he argues with justification that comedy about race is too complex a subject to regulate. In this respect he presents a strong counter-argument to the original proposition.

The weakness of the argument is that the author's position still leaves it wide open for people to be offended by racial humour. The 'right way' is not clearly defined, although there is a strong suggestion that he means by this 'done with irony', that is, you don't actually mean what you say. But who is to know whether the comic means it or not? Both Bernard Manning and Ali G are good examples of this. You can never be sure what their position is. To say it all depends on the context is fair enough, but what does this mean? Who is to decide whether the context is right or not? This is the weakness of the author's argument. It seems to boil down to a matter of personal opinion.

> **Examiner's comments**
>
> This is an excellent response, which does exactly what the question asks and assesses both the strength and weakness of the arguments in the passage. The student **goes straight to the point, identifies and analyses the key arguments, and provides references and reasons why these have been selected.**
>
> The response is **very specific and incisive**, and easily scores full marks by making sure that **at least three points are covered on each side** of the question.
>
> **The best responses often include the candidate's own viewpoints and references,** such as the comedy of Bernard Manning or Ali G referred to here.

3. Comedy is the business of making people laugh, essentially. Clinically speaking, laughing and smiling trigger one's brain to release endorphins which have the effect of killing pain and making one feel happier. Most people like to feel happy, so as comedy helps them, they like comedy.

As we have evolved to become an intelligent race, capable of serious thought and decisions, we have also developed the facility for entertainment. We cannot be hardworking and concentrating intensely for twenty-four hours a day, seven days a week. We need a break now and then, and often comedy gives us that break and the opportunity to relax and forget about daily problems.

Through comedy, we can laugh at embarrassing situations that may or may not have happened to us, and can accept that such things do happen and that we should not take ourselves too seriously. Many teen-comedy films such as 'American Pie' draw on the common experience of adolescence to provide humour from real life. Common life experience is a vital key to good comedy. Someone with no experience whatsoever of Asian families may not find humour in 'Goodness Gracious Me', but a show like 'Mr Bean' appeals to almost all audiences, as he stereotypes a person incapable of avoiding mishaps, which are common ground for most people. Some comedy can break through barriers of language and culture and bring people together – mime artists can perform anywhere in the world and be understood.

It is important to laugh *with* people of other cultures (and not to laugh *at* them) so that we understand those things we do have in common. There is room for the conveying of serious messages through comedy as well – role reversal of men and women challenging traditional stereotypes can be amusing and insightful, as it means that members of the audience are compelled to address their own stereotypical notions, perhaps. Comedians, such as Victoria Wood for example, poke fun at their own middle-class female stereotype, whilst deriding typical male behaviour at the same time.

In conclusion, comedy can aid the breaking down of barriers and acceptance of differences between people, but its main aim is simply to make us laugh and forget our troubles.

Examiner's comments

The examiner had no difficulty in awarding this response full marks. The key to its success is an appropriate range of general points, with appropriate and effective illustrations, which explained **the nature of different types of comedy and their appeal** – the essence of the question.

Amongst the points that could be included (many of which the student made, but not all) are that comedy

- represents an emotional and physical release and relief from tension
- takes us out of ourselves and enables us to forget our current problems and concerns
- can bring about physiological changes and have therapeutic effects (induces the release of endorphins – the body's natural pain-killer)
- often amuses through other people's misfortunes or foolishness, perhaps guarding against or excusing our own; we may be relieved that the discomfort it is not happening to us
- often amuses by unexpected turns of event or even words, in the case of verbal humour – many jokes are based on an element of surprise or irony.

The **range of types** could cover comedy of situation; character; slapstick; verbal humour, jokes and story-telling; satire. The **enjoyment that can be gained**: gentle amusement; appreciation of wit; uncontrollable 'belly-laugh'.

It is important to remember that you would not have to cover all of the above mark scheme points to gain full marks. This applies to most essay-type questions – **it is the overall quality of the response that counts.**

---

4. One of the basic human rights outlined in the constitutions of many democratic countries is freedom of speech and expression and a free press. These are embedded in the Human Rights Act (1998) in the UK and in the American Constitution, and in my opinion they are the most important rights besides the right to life. Freedom of speech is essential to a democratic, civilised society, as can be shown by the strict limits on these freedoms in countries with extreme left or right parties or dictators in power. For example there were many restrictions on broadcasting on radio and television in Afghanistan under the Taliban regime.

In my view censorship of the media by governments is a dangerous concept and one which should be exercised with caution. We should not be able to dictate what other people may write or say, or deny them the right to their own opinions or access to information. Yet there are clearly potentially damaging effects from total freedom in this area. There needs to be a degree of control since there are some people who wish to perpetuate bigotry and hatred by using lies and propaganda to convert others to their views. There is a need for 'facts' given in newspapers, textbooks and documentary programmes to be substantiated, and for redress when people are not telling the truth. I believe therefore that some restrictions are necessary and valid, but that these should be strictly limited and determined by an independent judiciary and not solely by the government in power.

It is also important to bear in mind that cultural values vary between groups and change over time. For example films censored in the 1950s would probably be treated differently today. It is right that performances and displays should be subject to regulation from an independent body, but the ways in which they are assessed, and under what criteria, should be kept under review to strike the right balance between the rights, freedoms and responsibilities of each individual.

When it comes to public performances for entertainment there is a need to consider the social context. The potential damage should be weighed against the effects of repression. People should not have to be exposed to things they do not wish to see, so there should be warnings about the content of particular publications and programmes, and there should be limits to what is shown and the time at which certain types of programmes are shown on free-to-air television, so that vulnerable groups are protected, like young children for example.

There is a difference also in my view between material that comes directly into people's homes, such as on the radio and free-to-air television, and what you have to go out of your way to buy or to see, for example as in pay-per-view programmes, or from shops in the form of books, magazines or videos, or in the cinema, theatre or clubs. I also agree with some legal restrictions on the age at which certain types of material can be seen or bought by young people. We do not exactly know whether very violent or sexually explicit films are harmful, so it is better to be cautious with young audiences and in some cases let parents decide, as they know their children best and what is suitable for them. Adults on the other hand should be able to decide for themselves whatever they wish to see, although I still think that there should be some regulation to stop things getting out of hand, such as opening up sex shops outside schools.

Examiner's comments

Despite finishing fairly abruptly, this answer gained full marks. The student **answered both parts of the question and did exactly what each part required.** He chose a **very good basic position,** which is to recognise the conflict of interests that censorship raises in an 'open and democratic' society, i.e.

- the right to freedom of expression, information and personal choice, *as opposed to*
- the right not be confronted by material you do not wish to see, which some people find upsetting or harmful.

It is possible to challenge the notion of the *absolute* right to be protected from, or denied access to, material that some may find offensive, at least for consenting adults. However, most people would accept that more vulnerable groups – such as children, old people, particular religious or cultural groups – might be entitled to a degree of consideration and protection when it comes down to choice of the material to be presented.

This leads to a possible argument that different measures may be appropriate to different circumstances, and these might relate to:

- the content and purpose of the material (humour and satire, serious social comment, displays of sexual or violent behaviour, and use of swearwords, etc.)
- the medium (TV – 'free-to-air', 'pay-per-view' – video, cinema, theatre, private club, literature, Internet)
- the audience (general, age-related, restricted, self-selected, exclusive).

There is also the question of who should determine what the public, groups or individuals are allowed to see or hear and in what circumstances:

- the law, politicians, appointed members of the British Film Classification Board, parents, producers, editors, pressure groups.

The notion that there should be no limits at all is a difficult one to sustain, but who should exercise the restraint and responsibility is probably more arguable. Some issues – such as libel, defamation, depraved material involving criminal acts, classified age limits – are properly covered by the law but others would be more appropriately left to the discretion and ethical judgements of responsible and accountable individuals, producers, editors, parents.

2 Science, Mathematics and Technology

Answers to multiple-choice questions (page 55)

Question	Correct answer	Examiner's hints
1.	B	**This is really a matter of fundamental knowledge**, but the answer can also be deduced from the equations in Figure 1a. There is also a significant reference to carbon dioxide emissions in the middle of paragraph 5. The key effect of using hydrogen is the reduction in the production of carbon dioxide (CO_2), which is a major greenhouse gas. B is the only sensible option here.
2.	C	Figure 1(a) tells you the amount of energy given out for one mole of each of the substances in the question. **Simple multiplication of the appropriate (ΔH) equation will lead you to the correct answer.** 1 mole of petrol would give out 5512 kJ mol^{-1}, 2 moles of methane 1780 kJ mol^{-1}, 10 moles of methanol 7150 kJ mol^{-1}, and 20 moles of hydrogen 5720 kJ mol^{-1}. 10 moles of methanol (answer C) therefore releases the most energy.
3.	B	Figure 1(c) tells you that methane produces four molecules of hydrogen for each molecule of methane, and methanol – which must be the alcohol referred to because you are directed to Figure 1(c) – only produces three. **Your own knowledge should tell you that water can produce only one molecule of hydrogen for each molecule of water** (because its formula is H_2O), and hydrogen (H_2) can have only one molecule per molecule. So, **since each molecule of methane (B) produces the greatest amount of hydrogen, it is the most efficient**.
4.	D	**You can deduce the answer from the information at the beginning and end of paragraph 4** – 'small, but wealthy island' effectively rules out Option 4, and 'wet, mountainous … fast-flowing rivers … uses only a tenth of its hydroelectric potential' supports Options 1 and 2. **You can also deduce from the remainder of the description** about Iceland and its keenness to develop hydrogen power that it does not have significant oil reserves – Option 3. So the answer is D.
5.	A	**Be careful not to leap too quickly here.** The key point about the hybrid technology is that it still produces carbon dioxide (end of paragraph 3), which rules out C. Water vapour *is* produced, and not producing global cooling is not an environmental benefit. The benefit in this case is just the reduction in nitrogen oxides (A).
6.	C	Once you have found the right information and interpreted it correctly, this is a simple calculation, but you have to **be careful about the number of 000s**. In the US 10% of cars are believed to produce 1 million tons of air pollutants per year. Therefore 100% would produce 10 million tons (C).
7.	D	Here you need some knowledge outside of the passage, which is why there is no paragraph reference, but **it is not unreasonable to expect that you will know what the anticipated consequences of global warming are. This is basic knowledge for General Studies**. Option 4 is a consequence of damage to the ozone layer, not global warming. You must know the difference.

8.	A	This also needs basic knowledge to answer, but **you should have covered it in GCSE Science**. The key word in the question is '**always**', which is why it is in bold type. A mixture of hydrogen and oxygen is potentially explosive, but not always – the test for hydrogen is that it will only explode if a spark or lighted flame is applied to it; whereas the other two options always apply as a matter of scientific fact.
9.	A	**The difference between fact and opinion, what is scientific proof etc., are key areas in General Studies** and questions about them will turn up frequently. A key element is that scientific theory and fact are **capable of being *dis*proved**, but have not been so far. Option 2 can be demonstrated by repeated experiment and therefore '**proved**'. Option 1 can not be stated as a fact – at this stage it can not be fully proved or disproved. It can only be an opinion, although it can be an 'informed' opinion. In fact combining hydrogen and oxygen produces water vapour, which is itself a greenhouse gas and a more powerful one than carbon dioxide! However, most of it would condense to liquid water, but potentially it could cause global warming. Statement 1 is actually an example of scientific dogma – the notion that carbon dioxide is the only factor in global warming.
10.	C	This final question brings together several points and **tests your logical powers as well as your comprehension of the passage**. As the question tells you, decide first of all if each statement is true. The assertion is true because there are fewer moving parts in the engine, and the reason is true because there is less need to overcome friction and less waste heat is generated. Now, decide whether the reason is a correct explanation. Here it is, because logically fuel cells are more efficient because of the reasons given, so the answer is C. This is supported by statements in paragraph 3.

Answers to short-answer and essay questions (page 57)

🎯 How to score full marks

1. By the media we could mean TV, radio and the press. Scientific stories are not widely reported in any of these (apart from specialist journals) unless there is a 'human interest' angle. One of the best-known examples is cloning and, since 1997, this has often meant *Dolly the Sheep*.

   Cloning is of major scientific importance. It involves stem cell research at its earliest stages (embryonic stem cells developed from human embryos). Scientists believe that *therapeutic cloning* may eventually replace damaged heart tissue and help people who suffer from degenerative diseases such as cystic fibrosis. However, some of the tabloids have concentrated on *reproductive cloning* – exaggerated, scare stories of 'designer babies' and even monsters.

   Research scientists often complain of incomplete or inaccurate reporting. In the case of the tabloids *Dolly the Sheep* more than justified the scientists' feelings.

   > **Examiner's comments**
   >
   > This was a slightly long answer for 5 marks but it clearly focused on the question and showed balance and restraint.
   >
   > The candidate's scientific knowledge was clear and well explained and the example used was highly topical.
   >
   > All the salient points were clearly made.

2. $5 + 7 = 12$ $11+13 = 24$ $17+19 = 36$ $23+29 = 52$ $31+37 = 68$

   > **Examiner's comments**
   >
   > Prime numbers are defined in the question. (Prime numbers cannot be divided exactly by any number other than 1.) A quick check reveals that the two primes used in each example are odd numbers greater than 3 and each answer gives an even number.

3. **(i)** The most effective way of defeating the dictator would have been for the general to divide his force into groups (1) so that the groups could advance along the many approach roads (1). Because the numbers in each group were small the mines did not explode (1). The general used a pre-arranged signal (1) thus allowing a co-ordinated attack by all groups at once (1). This was an effective strategy so victory was assured (1).

> **Examiner's comments**
> A logical and concise approach to the question. Marks awarded are shown (1).

  (ii) The major problem is that the question does not provided detailed information. It would have helped to know the size of the army, the state of communications, the possible counter-strategy of the dictator and the pattern/number of mines.

> **Examiner's comments**
> The candidate defined the problem and clearly identified four additional factors.

  (iii) The division of a large force into smaller ones that are easier to handle. This could apply to cancer radiotherapy, where several smaller rays could be directed to one place without damaging nearby healthy tissue.

> **Examiner's comments**
> Both the underlying principle and its wider application were clearly set out.

4. There is considerable pressure to conform to certain images – mostly those presented in health and fashion magazines – where the emphasis is on the 'tanned and the toned'. Fat is definitely unfashionable and 'lifestyle' has become a buzzword. Doctors and nutritionists are responsible for an endless stream of seemingly impeccably researched recommendations about diet and exercise. 'Healthy foods' abound in supermarkets.

Smokers get cancer and their lung capacity is much reduced. People who eat fatty foods get heart disease. Scientifically, the facts have been thoroughly researched and the evidence is overwhelming yet lots of people smoke despite the stark and unambiguous message on cigarette packets. The gym is part of life's fashion accessories yet many people lead the sedentary life of the couch potato in the style of TV's *The Royle Family*.

Like London taxi drivers, we have 'the knowledge' – which is of little value if we can't get our brains to send out messages that prompt the joints and muscles into activity. Fitness often means fulfilment – a better and healthier life. The problem is that when you're young you think you're untouchable, shielded from diseases other than coughs and colds. Serious illness is for old people. There's no real logic in that – it's just the belief that young people have.

It doesn't seem to matter that healthier people make fewer demands on the National Health Service. Most of us don't pay taxes and we make little use of the service. On reflection, it seems very selfish because we should be contributing to the good of the community. As teenagers we exist on coke and junk-food yet health education lessons make the consequences of such a diet clear. Obesity among young people is a growing trend. We are the ones who want to be cool and attractive, winning the approval of our peers.

I'm one of those seemingly unable to exercise free will. Put it down to laziness and complacency. Life expectancy continues to rise and gyms are full of TV sets to stop muscle bound men going out of their minds with boredom – or perhaps they need their daily fix of football and fast cars. Gyms are like human display counters – attractively packaged goods with a few reduced and bargain basement items. An hour's exercise a week among 7 days of unhealthy eating and driving everywhere.

Most girls can't wait for PE lessons to end – not that it's all muddy fields, cold legs, hard knocks and compulsory showers. Things are now a bit more enlightened which allows for an element of personal choice. Everyone is different and I'd certainly like to be a bit more healthy without becoming a lycra-clad fitness fanatic. Beauty is said to be 'in the eye of the beholder' and there should not be just one ideal of human perfection. A justification for being fat and frumpy? I'm just an A-level PE student and one of the girls in *Playing the Field*, a participant in the fastest growing sport – female football!

5. **(a)** When the word 'average' is used it is usually taken to be the 'mean average'. If there are four people in a group aged 16, 18, 20 and 22 the mean average is the sum of their ages (76) divided by the number in the group (4) – which is 19. Less commonly used are the 'median' (an average based on the middle number of a range of numbers) and the 'mode' (the most frequent number contained in a sequence).

Thus each of the three incomes can represent a different sort of average. Another possible explanation is that the incomes might be 'gross' (free of tax or other deductions) or 'net' (the amount left *after* tax and other deductions).

(b) Disraeli was a leading politician during the reign of Queen Victoria and politicians are very fond of using statistics. Mostly they use words but, in speeches or articles, statistics can be very useful to add support to what is being said or to 'prove' a point. Politicians need to convince people that they can help them to have a better standard of living and statistics can be used in this context – perhaps to show how much more money is being spent on services like health and education.

Used sparingly, simple statistics are much easier to understand than tables of data. Statistics can also add time comparisons so that politicians can seek to demonstrate, over time, how much their party is better, in terms of what it does or achieves, than opposing parties.

Statistics can also be powerful as well as useful. Politicians are often intoxicated by power and preoccupied by the means of holding on to it. Many people treat statistics as facts and, if properly researched – objectively and with reliable supporting evidence – they may be. Politicians can use statistics against opponents, perhaps illustrating fraud or a wasteful use of resources.

They are much in evidence at the time of the Budget when the Chancellor of the Exchequer uses statistics to reveal his plans for spending and raising money to the nation. In this sense, statistics can confirm relationships – perhaps between input and output in economic terms. They are also an excellent marketing tool in politics and other areas. Somebody with a good command of statistics, but not necessarily bound by the morality of truth, could sell almost anything to anyone.

Disraeli may well have been talking about an opponent when he linked statistics with lies and damned lies. When we use statistics we may make a presumption about what is 'normal' because it fits a statistical pattern. This would be a very narrow perspective on 'normality' and one which allows little for individual traits or idiosyncrasies. Similarly, as can be seen in the averages used in question (a), depending on the method used, the average for a set of figures can vary between £15,000 and £22,500.

Much depends on the motive of the user. The 'misleading' can be accidental because terms are not clearly defined, because the statistics have not been accurately combined or because the person using them does not know how to interpret them. Plenty of people besides politicians use statistics – advertisers make wide use of them. They can be used to mislead but this depends on many factors influencing the behaviour, and taking into account the motives, of the user. We must use statistics with care but used accurately and honestly their usefulness and power can outweigh the 'lies and damned lies'.

> **Examiner's comments**
>
> This was a very confident and well-written answer. It was not essential to use examples from politics simply because the source of the quote was a politician but, in the first part of the answer, politics provided a helpful context.
>
> The importance of correct methodology in gathering statistics was identified and the arguments were well balanced. The use and power of statistics was contrasted with the way in which carelessness, distortion or abuse can turn statistics into a negative force.
>
> Examples were provided, including an apt use of material from the first part of the question. The style was both fluent and coherent. The conclusion was clear and followed logically from the material that preceded it.

3 Science, Politics and the Economy

Answers to questions (page 78)

How to score full marks

1. (a) Consumer trends are changing patterns which can be identified by market researchers in the way that purchases make their choices and spend their money.

> **Examiner's comments**
>
> A full answer with marks for **changing patterns, identified by market researchers** and **the way that purchasers spend their money.**

(b) The spending power or shopping trends associated with people in their 50s or older.

> **Examiner's comments**
>
> The single sentence covers all necessary points.

(c) Industries that serve people, like shops will need to become more efficient because of competition from internet shopping.

> **Examiner's comments**
>
> Marks for **examples** of a service industry, greater efficiency and Internet competition.

(d) Convenience foods are more important for young people looking for a ready meal or for females who do not have a very active lifestyle.

> **Examiner's comments**
>
> Marks for **convenience foods, ready meal** and **non-active lifestyle.**

2. (a) D

> **Examiner's comments**
>
> $28.2 \times 12.8\% = 3\,609\,600$ men $+ 29.6 \times 18.5\% = 5\,476\,000$ women $= 9\,085\,600$ total

(b) Only the percentage of males over 65 has risen consistently between 1931 and 1998, suggesting that more men are living longer lives. There has been a very slight decline in the percentage aged 16–64 though the total number of men has risen. The Second World War, when many younger men were killed, may have influenced this. There is a more noticeable decline in the percentage aged under 16, although numbers in the group have increased slightly. This may reflect a more recent decline in the birth rate.

3. An immediate problem is that the table gives no information about the size of the different train operating companies so a comparison has very little value. The companies in the table are those which operate in London and the south-east of England. We cannot generalise and say that the same applies to all conurbations.

    It is now 2002 and the latest figures shown in the table are for 1998. Over the four years, the situation may have improved. Although the table is headed 'morning and evening rush-hours' we are not given a precise timescale for this. Although we can see that the service of some companies seems to have improved, while that of others has deteriorated, we are not given any reasons to account for this.

    To form reliable conclusions we need to have access to other types of knowledge.

4. A strength of this source is that it comes from *The Observer*, a respected broadsheet newspaper which provides serious reports and analysis of social issues. The language used by Richard Ellis is very powerful. Phrases like 'Britain is foul, racist and deeply prejudiced' are used to get the attention of the reader. Another strength is the extent that the reader is writing from experience. The title suggests that he is a white man married to a non-white woman and he will have seen prejudice at first hand. This personal experience of being in a mixed marriage allows the author to make a strong and persuasive case. In doing so he makes clear that racism can take several forms and that he has waited some time before writing the article to challenge what he calls 'a complacent liberal intelligentsia'. A further strength is the reference made to 'the Lawrence case' – a racist murder which received widespread national publicity.

    However, the source undoubtedly has weaknesses. Richard Ellis has clearly been personally affected by the experiences of his wife. This makes his writing subjective and one-sided in places. He also uses emotional language ('foul-mouthed, Union Jack-clad yob') and he may be prone to exaggeration. He writes in a newspaper known for its left-of-centre stance and one which is usually sympathetic to the causes of minorities. Despite the passion in the writing, there are sweeping generalisations (like the opening sentence). Many of the things he alleges may be justified but he does not seek to quantify the problem and he relies mainly on anecdotal evidence.

5. Much is made of predictions of global warming but, so far, the effects have been confined to trends such as warmer winters and earlier springs which don't affect people very much and are difficult to prove conclusively. The gradual thawing of polar ice caps seems serious to those with scientific knowledge but it is remote from the experience of the great majority of people. In terms of the overall impact of anti-pollution policies, the role and contribution of the individual seems infinitesimal especially if statistics cannot always be substantiated.

We must ask what motivates people in terms of how they make choices. Pollution is dangerous but its dangers are remote to those not directly affected or who have little real knowledge of the situation. Politicians claim to be in a position of power where they make decisions but, in the context of a global, multi-national economy the most powerful people are international capitalists – those who create wealth. The people who ask 'what effect will it have on me?' are likely to assume, in the short-term, that it will have very little unless they live close to dangerous industrial or traffic-based pollutants which can be measured.

Nevertheless, many people have more knowledge because they are better educated and scientific knowledge is more widely accessible. More people are concerned about the morality of pollution, especially if it is combined with exploitation. Satellite communications make us better informed about environmental disasters and green pressure groups like Friends of the Earth have been very effective in raising public awareness.

Knowledge is rarely 'certain' because it takes many forms, not all of which can be proved on a secure or consistent basis. There are grounds to be optimistic about the extent to which knowledge and awareness is increasing but it is not necessarily a case of what is, or isn't 'certain'. The extent to which people are well-informed about issues varies enormously and 'absence of certain knowledge' may not loom large in their calculations. What often triumphs, in reality, is self-interest over a wider sense of moral responsibility.

> **Examiner's comments**
> A sharp, balanced, and **critically written** answer, which **focused fully on the question** and **explored some of the different forms of knowledge and their limitations**. **Both sides of the question** were addressed to produce a 10-mark response which showed **full understanding of the limitations of statistical knowledge** and of the issues which may arise from the distinction between **fact and opinion**. Expression was **clear and logical**, with **no errors of significance in style or grammar**.

6. If I told you 'the truth' – and I'm told that a belief is true if it corresponds to the way the world is – about the drugs situation, you are likely to recoil in horror. Consider the second source. The writer is anonymous and anonymity hides all sorts of things. A product of the generation gap because he, or she, refers to grandchildren. Of course, it's nonsense to say that *all* drugs are harmful. There are plenty of drugs used by doctors which save lives. What the writer means are 'banned substances' – Class A and Class B stuff.

It's worth staying with the second source despite its generalisations. The writer has at least glimpsed something of the truth, if only on the estate concerned. The local police may well have published figures – officially endorsed, empirically gathered and close to the truth. But the writer has seen the truth all around – ' … discarded needles, closed-up shops, kicked in front doors'. As he or she (and perhaps it's a worried granny) says, 'drugs breed dependency and dependency leads to crime'. This is what she believes and to have a belief is to believe that the belief is true. More so if it corresponds with the facts.

I've seen *Trainspotting*. A bit worrying if you believe it will happen to you. Here's a contradiction. Most of us believe what *Trainspotting* showed was the truth about drugs. The truth on film. But we don't believe it can happen to us. We see the truth and reject it. As for London journalists, fiction is stranger than truth, to reverse a well-known saying.

Polly Toynbee might be offering her version of the truth just like I'm offering mine. Mo Mowlam? If politicians told the truth nobody would ever vote for them because the truth can be unpalatable. It hurts. The Drugs Tsar? If Keith Halliwell wants to keep his job he might have to bear this is mind. Conservative drugs policy? I suppose it's another version of what they see as the truth based on belief. If you believe deterrence deters. Only in the case of execution and then just for the individual concerned. Drugs are rife in most prisons. Home Office figures tell the truth. What Hague believes is false because it does not match the facts.

No doubt Polly Toynbee overstates her case to make an impact. It's not true that 'all politicians … lie brazenly'. Some might get quite near the truth. (Look in *Hansard*.) I agree that 'some say what they plainly cannot believe' because they want to stay in a job. That means saying what most of their electorate want to hear. Telling lies really but, skilfully done, it looks like the truth. That's how life operates. Moral dilemmas to be solved. Feelings to be protected. If you can trust the pollsters – and their methods are usually scientific – it's true to say that more and more younger people don't bother to vote. But how do you explain this? That would be a really interesting search for the truth if I had more time.

Does either source tell the truth? The truth, the whole truth and nothing but the truth? Of course not. There are elements of truth – beliefs fully supported by facts, plus assertions, fallacies, opinions etc. The Americans use truth drugs. Watch out Polly Toynbee.

> **Examiner's comments**
>
> An **unusual style** but the first sentence, which offers a **limited definition of truth** is indicative of the quality of content. The answer recognised the potential weaknesses of the second source (e.g. **generalisation**) but it recognises where the truth might appear, even pointing out the irony of seeing but rejecting the truth. The first source is used to extend the definition of truth (**beliefs supported by facts**). **Methods of establishing the truth** are mentioned, as is the quest for **interpretation of evidence**. The difficulties are highlighted in the conclusion – **truth** mixed with **assertions, fallacies** and **opinions**. A bold and challenging style but a **highly informed analysis** of considerable merit.

7. That there is no real difference between the Labour, Conservative and Liberal Democrat parties is a common assertion. In terms of ideology there may be some support for this point of view. Less than 20 years ago, the Labour Party was felt to be 'unelectable' when its policies and leadership were to the left of centre. The party was identified with unpopular policies such as support for trade unions, nationalisation and unilateral nuclear disarmament. Under the Conservatives, well to the right of centre, under Margaret Thatcher and free market ideas there were significant differences between the parties.

During the 1980s, a reform movement developed within the Labour Party, first under Neil Kinnock and then John Smith. When the latter died suddenly, Tony Blair became leader. His party swept to power with a landslide victory in 1997 – a feat that was repeated in 2001. These were triumphs for what became known as 'New Labour' – more apart from the trade unions, business friendly and willing to allow the private sector to take more of a role in the provision of public services. The Conservatives, under William Hague and Iain Duncan Smith, complained that Labour had stolen many of their ideas.

Many 'Old Labour' supporters are critical of the party's more recent stance which they see as right wing compared, say, to the policies of Attlee's 1945–51 Labour government which was responsible for a huge expansion of the welfare state, including the setting up of the National Health Service. New Labour supporters argue that the change was necessary. Traditional Labour voters were disappearing as unionised jobs in heavy industry were swept away along with streets of terraced housing. To gain electoral success, Labour had to appeal to a much wider range of voters – many of whom were, or aspired to be, middle class. To do so, and to win the support of a largely Conservative supporting national press, Labour did appear to become more like the Conservatives – although some would argue that it simply became more conservative and less willing to take risks.

The Conservatives had no answer to this. Margaret Thatcher captured the popular mood in the 1980s when privatisation and the modernisation of industry seemed to have great support. By the 1990s, there was a wider realisation that individual freedom also brought misery in terms of unemployment and the break-up of communities, both of which increased social problems. Labour moved to the more 'central' political ground that the Conservatives had deserted. The Conservatives had nowhere to go, unless it was further to the right. A divided party, it became more Euro sceptic and took a hard line on social problems which appeared to do little to tackle their causes. The popular mood had changed and Labour, with its careful planning and consummate spin doctoring of communications, caught this new mood.

The Liberal Democrats, very much a 'third party' in terms of its number of MPs was a beneficiary of the change and the tendency towards 'tactical voting' – which essentially meant keeping out the Conservatives at all costs. Over 50 Liberal MPs were in Westminster after the 1997 Election; the number increasing slightly in 2001. Ironically, it was widely felt that, as Labour moved to the centre, the Liberal Democrats under Paddy Ashdown and Charles Kennedy moved towards at least some former Labour ground to the left of centre.

There are differences between the three largest parties, particularly over Europe, immigration and the provision of public services. These differences are not as pronounced as they were in the 1980s but it might be argued that, if the parties did not have a distinctive outlook, the results of the last two general elections would have been much closer. That they were not suggests that many voters are aware of the differences and that they find 'New Labour' and, to a lesser extent, Liberal Democrat policies so clearly preferable is a reflection of this.

Examiner's comments

This was the answer of a **politically literate** candidate who knew that the key words were **critically examine** rather than 'agree with' or 'describe'. The first sentence **identified** the three largest British political parties and each paragraph that followed was **clearly linked** and written without recourse to **political jargon** or **slogans**. A clear **contrast** was made between **New Labour** and **Old Labour**, showing how and why **ideologies** and **policies** had changed. Comparisons were made with the **changing position of the Conservative Party**, and the rise of the **Liberal Democrats** in the 1990s was charted. The **conclusion** was interesting, **clearly expressed** and linked to the **evidence** and **arguments** contained in the main body of the essay.

---

8. **(a)** Social benefits are paid to different groups of people who qualify to receive them because they have made National Insurance contributions or because they are said to 'need' the benefits by meeting certain qualifying conditions. Most benefits are paid by the government through The Benefits Agency but some are paid by larger councils.

People with very low incomes often qualify for housing benefit from their councils to help with the payment of their rent and rates. Job Seeker's Allowance is paid to certain categories of those who are unemployed and seeking work. Those unable to work might qualify for Incapacity Benefit if they are unable to work because of an illness. Child Benefit is paid to support each child and is not based on any contributions.

Examiner's comments

Two paragraphs of continuous prose are all that is required for the 'lead in' section, where there are only 10 (out of 50) marks. Benefits were **clearly explained** and four sentences were used to **identify** and **describe** examples to support the answer.

(b) It is not unusual to see headlines in some newspapers which give the impression that almost everyone who receives a social benefit is a scrounger who cheats the system. Often these 'scroungers' come into certain categories, most notably young people who do not work and asylum seekers. While there are undoubtedly those who seek to cheat the system, it is unfair and inaccurate to stereotype people who have a genuine need and who are only claiming benefits to which they are entitled.

The critics are often those who have never needed benefits or who have no knowledge of those who do. I am a mature student seeking to gain extra qualifications to go to university. I have worked for the Benefits Agency. This may make me biased but it also means that I have experience and understanding of the system. One thing I can say is that it is far more difficult to cheat the system than is often imagined. Newspaper campaigns warn people about making false claims and the Investigations Branch is very active. Cheats and scroungers can certainly be prosecuted and, in the worst cases, sent to prison.

What we often forget is that the great majority who receive benefits are old people who need their pensions and the many disabled people who might want to work but who are unable to do so. Old people, in particular, are not usually classed as scroungers. Indeed, many do not claim all the benefits they are entitled to because 'being on benefit' used to be a real stigma in their younger days. It was made to seem more like charity and made a lot of people feel ashamed.

It is often assumed that many of the unemployed are 'workshy'. Some almost certainly are but there are parts of the country, especially in parts of Northern England and South Wales, where job opportunities are very limited and often poorly paid. Benefits are set at a fairly low level but sometimes they can be higher than the very low wages paid in some parts of the country – something the national minimum wage is trying to tackle.

We are also given the impression that the benefits system is overrun by asylum seekers who come to Britain mainly for the 'generous' social security which is 'easy to obtain'. In my experience, nothing could be further from reality. The process for claiming benefits which asylum seekers have to go through is complicated and those who get them are paid at a very low level. Perhaps it was because of distorted press coverage that the government decided to pay part of the (very small) benefits in vouchers which could only be spent in certain shops – another example of trying to stigmatise those in need, though, belatedly, vouchers have now been abandoned.

If people have paid National Insurance contributions during their working lives they are *entitled* to benefits at certain times in their lives. It is like any other form of insurance – to protect us at times of risk and vulnerability (when we are ill or old). Some people can afford to do this for themselves or to take out private insurance. This is their choice but many do not have enough money to make that sort of choice.

Other benefits are paid for out of taxation. I don't like the thought of the tax I pay going to those who don't deserve the benefits it pays for. I would like there to be an ideal system which ensures that benefits only go to those who are entitled to them. In real life this is not possible. The system we have is very complicated to administer and nobody can provide a 'cheat proof' system.

When I was much younger I remember seeing a TV play called *Scroungers*. It was written by a man called Jim Allen on a kitchen table in a Manchester council house. Perhaps it is only fiction but the more detailed reports of those who investigate and record poverty and causes would back it up. I wish the BBC would show it again to make some people think a bit more.

I don't deny that there are scroungers and that the system is sometimes cheated. If the rules were made even harsher there would be even fewer cheats – an aim that most people would support. A far bigger problem than cheating is making sure that people claim the benefits which are theirs by right. A great many don't. Harsher rules would make this situation far worse. This won't make tabloid headlines but, without the existence of the benefit system, we would cease to be a humane society trying to protect vulnerable people who exist in far greater numbers than the cheats and scroungers.

Examiner's comments

This was an outstanding answer with many strengths. The mature student who wrote it had **knowledge gained through experience.** However, the issue often produces a very **subjective** and often **emotional** response where there is far more **opinion** than **rational and substantiated analysis.**

While this answer showed some **personal feelings** it was nearly always **detached** and **soundly argued.** It brought out the **complexities** of the problem and indicated that such problems are **never likely to have simple solutions.** The dangers of **stereotyping** were clearly identified, as were the dangers of **acquiring knowledge and making judgements** solely on the basis of one-sided newspaper reports. The **fact** that there are scroungers was not challenged. What was questioned seriously was our lack of ability to **quantify** the problem and the issues associated with **stigmatising** those **genuinely in need** and **entitled to benefit.**